Overcoming Guilt and Shame

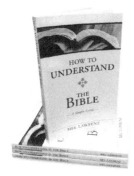

Overcoming Guilt and Shame

DANIEL GREEN, PH.D.
MEL LAWRENZ, PH.D.

WWW.WORDWAY.ORG

Acknowledgments

Long before any of the ideas in this book were committed to paper, they were developed at length with our wives, Lynne and Ingrid. The contents of this work owe much to the creative work invested by our life partners.

It was a privilege to develop and test these ideas with our colleagues at New Life Resources, Inc. and at Elmbrook Church. They know that guilt and shame are recurring issues in both pastoral ministry and professional counseling. Our colleagues are looking for good answers to the pressing questions we all have, and helped us keep this work practical and meaningful.

We are also thankful for the numerous contributions offered by the many Elmbrook Christian Study Center students who participated in a class titled "Guilt and Shame in Christian Perspective." Their insights, questions, and feedback sharpened our understanding and were much appreciated.

CONTENTS

1

Why Do I Feel Like Hiding?

I sometimes think that shame, mere awkward, senseless shame, does as much towards preventing good acts and straightforward happiness as any of our vices can do.

— C.S. Lewis

The young man swallowed hard, moistening his mouth so that when he spoke his tongue would not stick to the inside of his mouth. He was aware that his heart was racing and that his breathing was shallow. He thought to himself, I've got to get a different job or convince my boss that I can't make presentations like this. As he began to speak, he felt like every eye in the room was peering through him, and the sensed that they could see him for the fake he thought he was. *I'm a nobody, and I've got nothing to say.*

It did not help when he returned to his office to find a file on his desk of a transaction from two years past, reminding him of the cheating he had done to pull the deal off. He felt flushed and noticed the familiar knot in his stomach that came whenever he was face to face with the seedier side of his professional life. He wondered whether his conscience was a blessing or a curse. Other piles of papers on his desk reminded him of how unproductive he had been for the past six months, and he wondered whether everyone in the office looked at him as a total failure.

He returned home in the hope that things would be fairly peaceful, and that he would be able to turn off the painful feelings of another stressful day. He was practically oblivious to his two-year-old daughter stretching out her arms to her daddy. A moment later, he glanced down and noticed she now stood very still, arms at her side, glancing towards the floor. He thought the way she looked was the way way he felt.

He told his wife that night that he thought he needed to get some things straightened out in his life. He did not know what or how. All that he knew was that he felt like he was hiding from something—or was it from everything?—because he felt small before other people, ashamed of himself, unjustified in his very existence before God.

IT'S NOT JUST YOU

We all experience guilt and shame. Living as members of a fallen race in a fallen world has made it inevitable that we will have to deal with being wrong and feeling wrong at different times. We all go through our own internal ways of checking our attitudes or actions. Most people experience an inner conflict when they know that what they do or say is "wrong" by some internal set of standards. There are any number of different ways in which we react. Sometimes we try to change our behaviors, other times we adjust our standards to try to justify ourselves. And there is always the possibility that we will just try waiting the feeling out.

There is a whole range of experiences in which we feel ashamed. If our consciences are intact, we will feel ashamed when we violate God's standards. Then again, we may experience shame apart from any moral violation on our part. From the simple embarrassment of realizing you put on two different colored socks, to the remorse for having disappointed a friend, to the mortification of being belittled by a parent, we routinely experience the sense of incompleteness or disconnection that comes from living in a disconnected world.

Susan had tried many times to describe it. The hard part was understanding it. It seemed like nothing and like everything—a feeling of incompleteness and hollowness that dogged her everyday. On better days it was like a grey cloud, robbing her of joy and pleasure, but on the bad days she felt like she was looking out of a long dark tunnel with a mere pinpoint of light at the end. It was almost unbearable to be around other people, because then she sensed how inept she felt, how klutzy, how foolish. She would avoid saying much because when she did she always worried that she had said the wrong thing. Everything in her told her to run away and hide. And then there was her family. What kind of a mother, what kind of wife can I claim to be, she thought. They'd all be better off without me. When her husband tried to help, she only ended up feeling worse for being such a bother. She felt like there was a wide canyon between her and everybody in her life. She felt disconnected from virtually everybody.

Some people, like Susan, feel trapped in prisons of shame. Their experience goes way beyond the ordinary field of play of the conscience. It's not just that they "feel guilty" about some things, they feel it about everything. It can get to the point where they no longer even think in terms of guilt. All they know is that all of life looks foreboding; they feel incapable of handling any kind of life challenge; they certainly do not feel up to handling relationships with others.

This book is for anyone who is looking for an answer to these questions: How can I get past my guilt? How can I become less ashamed? How can I know when I am really guilty before God and when not? Why do I feel so wrong when there is no apparent cause? How can some people do things that are so hurtful and not feel ashamed at all? Where do guilt and shame figure into the Christian life? Are Christians supposed to feel guilty all the time because they are sinners?

WHAT IS SHAME?

Shame is an emotion. It may or may not be related to something specific you do. It may come unexpectedly. It may be a constant, relentless voice shouting words of self-condemnation, or it may be a subtle whisper. It may be helpful, or it may be destructive. As one of the most basic emotions that we experience, like anger or joy or sadness, shame is simply our internal reaction to things going on around or inside us.

What is it that prompts a blushing face? Mark Twain said that human beings are the only kind of animals who blush—or need to. That flushed face says that there is a rush of inner, conflicting feelings, a mild or strong sense of shame. The fair-skinned really talented blushers of this world have this facial readout that tells everyone around them, "I'm ashamed right now!" Blushers do not necessarily like blushing. But don't we all like blushers all the more for his or her blushing? Any honest person will think, "even though my face doesn't show it, I often feel the same way that person looks." Maybe it was because you said something you wish you could take back, maybe because someone humiliated you in public, then again that racing heart may come when someone says something good about you, and though that feels good, it also brings the embarrassment of being in the limelight, of being exposed.

Then there is the bowed head. What do we do when we are ashamed? We turn our eyes downward, avoiding eye contact as a part of withdrawal or hiding. We might even hang our heads. As an attempted solution, we speak of "saving face." You can even see some people pulling their heads backward rigidly, trying to look unabashed. If someone has ever told you to "keep your chin up" it is because they do not want to become fixed in a stance of shame. No one wants to suffer the indignity of "losing face." We might even try pasting on a look of contempt, or just freeze the face in an emotionless mask. To let others know that we feel ashamed will only add shame on top of shame. Some hide behind performance. If the ego is threatened with shame, the person goes to work, doing that function or playing the role that has always scored points with others. For Adam and Eve it meant hiding amidst the trees of the garden.

Shame results from disconnection. To understand this, first think of what it means to have a "connected" life, that is, one in which there is an active relationship with other people and with God, when there is an inner unity or harmony within the self. Connection is essential to a healthy life. It involves a meeting of hearts, an openness and vulnerability, a giving and receiving, a recognition and responsiveness to the other person, and communication that the person is valuable. Connection includes being touched, heard, and seen. Emotions are involved when two people connect, for we only connect at points of vulnerability. The scriptural principle of *reconciliation* is really the same as connection. Reconciliation is the *reconnection* that may occur where there is healing of a disconnection of two parties.

Contrast this with the state of disconnection, of being cut off from others and disjointed within yourself. What triggers shame in us is that experience of getting cut off or disconnected. Shame serves as a kind of emotional alarm. It signals the inherent danger of isolation and alienation. This can be an external threat (the outside accuser) or an internal one (an inner voice of self-condemnation). People can actually be their own worst enemies if the self hates the self.

Shame also serves to warn a person that to remain vulnerable may not be safe in a given situation. The person who inadvertently says the wrong thing in a social setting, the young child who misbehaves and disappoints his or her parents, and the individual who is confronted in front of colleagues regarding inadequate performance share a common experience. The pain of the shame serves to steer them away from further inappropriate acts and thus protects from further harm. In addition, thoughts, feelings, needs, wants, and events that occur during a shame experience are joined or paired with the emotion of shame. For example, if as a child you were made to feel ashamed whenever you got angry, then as an adult the emotion of shame comes right along whenever anger occurs. If these pairings occur frequently or if the emotional intensity of the shame is high, the later occurrence of the thought, need, want, or event will elicit the feeling of shame and the corresponding sense of disconnection, pain, and inhibition.

Psychologists point out that this whole spectrum of feelings in which a person feels like pulling back or hiding is a single kind of emotion. "Shame" is a good description of this range of feelings, which all have in common the sense of being disconnected from someone else, of feeling as though you don't measure up, and thus the need to withdraw or hide. It includes remorse and regret, but also self-contempt or self-hatred, and, in a much milder form, simple shyness and embarrassment.

Shame may come when we really did something wrong, and in this instance is a God-given friend who is warning us of the dangers of moral violation—or it may come when someone else has imposed an unfair and critical judgment on us. We see it all the time, people controlling other people through belittling and depreciating. Here shame is the unfortunate wound of a vulnerable conscience. In both instances the feeling is the same in kind. The victim of rape may deal for a long time with the shame of feeling less as a person, but the rapist, in some cases, may go through the shame of remorse. Both are ashamed, but for entirely different reasons, requiring totally different responses. This is the great challenge: How do we discern the difference between times when shame is a friend, and when it is an unwelcome intruder.

Some people deal with shame in an average kind of way. In the course of a day they may feel remorse for having been too harsh with the children, then embarrassed when they accidently walked out of the store without paying for an item, then just basically discouraged because they were able to accomplish only half of what they wanted to in the day.

For others shame has become the crippled posture of their lives. They live constricted lives because no matter where they turn or what they do they feel ashamed. They are offered a promotion at work, and they have a sense of dread that they will not be able to live up to expectations, they fuss about their appearance, always feeling like people are seeing them as slovenly, and then when they do make a mistake, even a simple one, they spiral downward in a dark tunnel of shame, sure that others now know just what rotten people they are. Shame itself can trigger more shame, resulting in an ever-louder voice of condemnation. Not surprisingly, a person bound by shame in this way was probably profoundly influenced by the demeaning behaviors of others earlier in life.

WHAT IS GUILT?

In its primary sense "guilt" is not a feeling, but a status. We determine guilt with our thinking capabilities, making judgments about the behavior of ourselves or of others. Because we have concepts like "guilty," and its opposite, "innocence," we can make moral judgments in life. We can seek to do the "right thing" and hope that the other guy does right by us.

"Feeling guilty" in many instances is not the problem, but the occasion for change. We do not like the feeling; we want to get past it. There is nothing surprising there. But whereas one person needs to get out from under the unfair false accusations of others, another needs to correct a situation where he or she is morally responsible.

In this day and age we tend to concentrate on the subjective. People sometimes are more concerned about the issue of feeling guilty than being guilty. Yet consider the courtroom. If you are a defendant in a trial, you know that there will be one of two outcomes. You will either walk freely out of the court if the judge or jury returns a "not guilty" verdict, or you will fall under the sanctions of the court if pronounced "guilty." The issue is solely that of whether you violated the standards of an objective rule, the law. So should we evaluate many of our actions on a day-by-day basis.

If someone has great emotional distress because he bought stock with inside information, the issue is not just how he is going to deal with his feelings, but how he will judge his actions. If a husband is laden with shame because his wife is blaming him for everything that is wrong in their marriage, he needs to sort out where he has been guilty and where not. The teenager, who tells her parents not to lay one more "guilt trip" on her, needs not just to react to her parents' voice, but also to figure out whether there is any truth in their judgment of her actions.

Look in almost any dictionary and you will find the original objective idea of guilt. One dictionary defines guilt as "the *fact* of being responsible for an offense or wrongdoing." Only *secondarily* does it list "remorseful awareness of having done something wrong or of having failed to do something required or expected." The imposing Oxford English Dictionary overwhelmingly stresses the objective sense of guilt: it is "a failure of duty, delinquency; offense, crime, sin; responsibility for an action or event; the fact of having committed some specified or implied offense; criminality; culpability." Guilt begins as a question of status. Am I guilty or not? Is someone else besides me the actual guilty party? Thus the opposite of guilt is innocence, not the feeling of having a clear conscience. Haven't we all met people whose consciences do not bother them, but they are plenty guilty?

We get this notion of guilt from biblical truth. The whole point of the sacrificial system in the Old Testament and the forgiveness offered us through the cross of Christ is that God has provided ways for us to get out from under a verdict of "guilty." Dealing with the associated feelings is a part of the process to be sure, for the Scriptures talk about having your conscience cleaned and made pure. But it all has to begin with a solution for the fact of being sinners and the fact of having sinned.

GETTING OUR THINKING STRAIGHT

Guilt and shame are fundamental biblical principles. The Scriptures show us the connection between the two. The story of Eden tells us of things that are basic to life, and there we find the first instance of guilt, and its immediate result—shame. "The man and his wife were both naked, and felt no shame" (Gen. 2:25). Yet, after the sin of taking forbidden fruit they take the characteristic posture of shame—hiding.

> *The man and his wife hid themselves from the presence of the LORD God among the trees of the garden. But the LORD God called to the man, and said to him, "Where are you?" He said, "I heard the sound of you in the garden, and I was afraid, because I was naked; and I hid myself" (3:8-10).*

In the modern world we tend to think the first question is, "Where is God?" whereas the more original question belongs to God: "Where is man?" What happened? Why are you hiding? Obscurity is a game human beings play with God, not the other way around. Shame does not exist in a vacuum. When people experience shame, they have a sense of disgrace about something, and before someone. It is from the displeasure of God that Adam and Eve hide themselves, and so it is with everyone who is guilty but neglects going with a contrite heart to the offended. They end up more estranged. Shame snuffs out the living warmth of relationships. In the second generation (Cain and Abel), and ever since, we see the disintegrating effects of human relationships and human/divine relationships all because of guilt and shame.

It is desperately important that when we try to understand our guilt and shame we not look at part of the puzzle isolated from the whole. Many people are in a desperate search for relief from the chronic feelings of pained consciences. They just want not to "feel so guilty." But if we only consider our feelings apart from the objective issues of whether we *are* guilty, we may miss the very solution to the problem. After all, the problems of the human race began when the first generation *did* something wrong.

On the other hand, someone's problems with guilt or shame may not be addressed at all by simply assuming that the person "blew it" somewhere and he or she needs just to look hard enough to find his or her guilt. Job's counselors probed around, trying to find out where he had transgressed against God, totally missing the point that Job was feeling so low simply because of the pain and losses in his life.

Before we go on to further descriptions of guilt and shame in our lives and how to find solutions, we would do well to clarify in our thinking the way all these different pieces of the puzzle fit together. In the ups and downs of life it is possible for us to get confused, as was the case with Job. Afflicted in body and demoralized by personal loss Job could not figure out whether he was to blame or not: "If I am guilty—woe to me! Even if I am innocent, I cannot lift my head, for I am full of shame and drowned in my affliction" (10:15). Job did not know whether he was guilty or not (his "friends" blamed him, but Job had his doubts), all he knew was that he *felt* tremendous shame.

In this book when the word "guilt" is used, it is referring to that primary historic sense of the word: the fact of having done something wrong. It is not the feeling of having done something wrong (which ordinarily is the emotional by-product of being guilty). It is making a mistake (not the feeling of being mistaken), breaking a law (not the feeling of remorse), violating a command of God (not the feeling of standing condemned before God). If we do not preserve this key concept of *status* we will make it very hard ultimately to find the peace of a cleansed conscience.

"Shame," on the other hand is that whole experiential side of things, the emotion that is prevalent when we feel small, disconnected, limited, or fallible. Psychologists observe that this class of emotions has the common characteristic of wanting to withdraw or hide. From embarrassment, to remorse, to mortification—there is that common reflex of pulling back because we sense a disconnection.

It will help us tremendously to speak of *being* guilty but *feeling* shame. When we speak of "feeling guilty" all the time, we run the risk of confusing the issue of status with that of experience. We might try to deal with the feeling and not the cause, which is like trying to put out a fire by shooting water at the tips of the flames. It is socially acceptable to talk about "feeling guilty" for not writing a letter in return, or eating ice cream too often, or spending more on clothes than we intended to. If life's issues were not more complicated than these, perhaps it would not matter how we speak of it. But we need to get down to serious solutions when the issue is the shame following an illicit affair, or the shame of being beaten by your husband, or of having a chronic illness.

That is when we need all the careful biblical distinctions that help us understand our true status before God and others, and our inner experiences. Indeed, the Bible itself probably has no page where guilt and shame are not directly or indirectly addressed. In the chapters that follow, we will further elaborate on the subtle but important differences in how we experience shame and how we perceive guilt. "Guilt" is simply the issue of whether or not we are in the wrong. Our experience, on the other hand, the "shame" that we feel, has many different subtleties. We might distinguish between three different forms of shame: *moral, imposed,* and *natural* shame (see table 1.1).

Table 1.1
Brief Definitions

Guilt: the fact of wrongdoing, being in the wrong

Moral shame: regret or remorse for having done wrong

Imposed shame: disgrace or devaluation inflicted by another

Natural shame: a sense of limitation, fallibility, humility

So many of the contemporary issues that come and go are really the issue of guilt and shame in other terms. People who are seeking what they call better *self-esteem* are really struggling with real or imagined guilt, or one of the forms of shame. Much attention is being given to *addictions*, the familiar chemical addictions like drugs or alcohol, and now certain compulsive behaviors related to eating or sex. If all addictions, no matter how we understand them, are attempts to escape or cover over some inner pain, might it not be that that pain is guilt or shame? Another common contemporary issue is relationships. We were created to live in relationship. Guilt and shame are the reasons people sense that they are distant from God and alienated from each other. We will have better relationships only if we can consistently deal with the mistakes and sins we commit (guilt), and understand the dynamics of shame that, by its very nature, is a separation between persons.

If guilt and shame are obvious universal human predicaments (and psychology has only further confirmed their universality), then the Christian gospel offers the only comprehensive solution to all manifestations of guilt and shame. To put it in a nutshell: the Christian gospel offers forgiveness for guilt, cleansing of conscience for moral shame, vindication for imposed shame, and acceptance of the person in the face of natural shame. This message of salvation in the broad sense, is further validated by the Christian view of sin, which is the only realistic way of sizing up who we are, where we are responsible, and where lie the faults of others as well. Because there is an antidote—a complete and effective antidote—it is not unbearable to look at the problems in us and in others.

2

So What's the Verdict on Me?

Laura had dared talk to only three people she could trust: her husband, her best friend, and her pastor. What her heart longed to know is whether she had sinned in such a way that now she was going to be rejected by God. She felt responsible for all the distresses her family had gone through lately. Her mother and father were getting a divorce, her husband had discovered he had a bleeding ulcer, and their oldest daughter seemed to be turning into some kind of recluse.

She actually felt frustrated that she got the same kind of response from all three confidants; they didn't see anything that she had done or was doing that was the direct cause of the problems, and they certainly didn't agree that she had reason to fear God's rejection. Yet she kept on searching: What have I done? What should I do?

Mark was a promising new addition to the firm—bright, talented, and ambitious. Yet three weeks into the position his boss noticed a disturbing trend. Whenever a problem arose in Mark's area he never took any responsibility for it. His typical response was to blame other people, and if that didn't work, he would minimize the problem. His boss tried to impress on him the importance of such mistakes, but then Mark would act as if it was his boss's problem. One month into the new job he had already lost the respect of everybody who worked around him, yet he barely noticed. What nobody in the office knew was how much worse he treated his wife. He would belittle her in public, berate her in private, and basically expect her to meet his every need. After less than a year of marriage she had given up telling him her hurts. The day his mother called her and blasted her for not taking good enough care of Mark, Mark's wife decided she needed to talk to someone for advice.

We know life is complex when we meet people like Laura—those who think they are guilty when they are not—and Mark—those who think they are innocent when they are not. It's not the way our sensibilities are supposed to work. Yet, living in a fallen and imperfect world, we will constantly have to sort out the truth of such matters. We have to learn how God views us all.

LOOKING GUILT IN THE EYES

How do I know when I'm guilty? Some people ask themselves that question frequently, some hardly at all.

Unfortunately, oftentimes those who don't ask it are the ones who should, while those who agonize over it have gotten guilt confused with the experience of shame.

Sometimes we *feel* ashamed as a result of *being* guilty. That is the way things should work in the human conscience. But, because we are complex and fallible creatures, that does not always happen.

Remember, the primary meaning of "guilt" is to be at fault. This issue of status is an issue distinct from experiences of thought and emotion we have. We have to deal not just with *feeling* or *thinking* we are wrong, but whether or not we are wrong in a given situation. In this chapter we'll focus on the question of guilt before going on to our emotional experience—our shame—in subsequent chapters. There are several important reasons for doing this.

If we are experiencing feelings related to guilt or shame and are searching for a possible fault in ourselves, we need to have a clear idea of what constitutes a real fault, mistake, or sin. Amazingly, some people think that wearing a color that your spouse does not like is a wrong, and others convince themselves that they are perfectly justified in getting into an adulterous affair.

In the course of normal events, we will frequently have to judge the actions of others. This is not being judgmental; it is the ordinary discernment that we all have to exercise. A parent needs to decide whether a child who refuses to get dressed is testing the authority of the parent, or is simply tired or sick. If someone tells you that you are being taken advantage of by someone else, you have to examine what has been going on, and ask yourself if you have been wronged. If you find yourself increasingly irritated with your spouse you have to decide whether your spouse has been sinning against you or whether it is merely personal differences that are causing some friction. Maybe you'll realize that it has nothing to do with your spouse, but that you have been transferring onto your spouse irritations that are coming from your job or your kids.

We need to understand guilt because we will be faced with decisions that are tough moral choices, and it is best to make them with our eyes open rather than being surprised by shame later on. Here is the parent who, after months of agonizing conflict, tells his teen-age kid that he cannot have the benefits of living in the house unless he seeks treatment for his drug abuse; or the manager who knows he has to fire an employee who is trying his best but is not able to do the job. Here is the family who knows that they are going to be going through pangs of conscience for putting their mother in the nursing home, even though that is the only viable option they have. Just because it is difficult to do something does not mean it is wrong.

Living in the modern world is not easy. We need some way of understanding guilt because having moral guidelines in our lives is the only way to live a healthy and whole life. Human beings left to their own inclinations do not naturally seek morally correct patterns for living. Sometimes social norms are helpful to people looking for moral definitions, but we cannot assume any such thing in the modern world. For some, the only absolute truth there is, is that there is no absolute truth. Yet how many of us would be comfortable with the notion that we can do without the protection of the laws of the land, for instance. No, the only way to have order and not anarchy in our lives is to have some moral structure to which we can apply the many decisions we face day in day out.

If we love God, we will want our lives to be ordered according to his desires. Learning about doing what is right in God's eyes involves learning also what is wrong. Some people have bad memories of teachers or parents or bosses who never told them what they were doing right, but attacked them when they did wrong. Others have the disappointing experience of being neither affirmed nor corrected, but just ignored. God treats us in neither way. The Bible, as the expression of God's will, is a positive statement of what it means to be right and do right. It contains correctives as well, but not without the promise of God's enabling. The fact that he made us moral creatures at all places on us a great responsibility (even though some would say burden), as well as a great privilege. What an amazing thing it is to be the only creatures in creation who have a sense of ought and ought not; of good, better, and best; of right and wrong; of innocence and guilt.

There are other reasons for looking the issue of guilt straight in the eye, but if we took just these we can see that living life would be an impossible task if we tried to pretend guilt and innocence were not real issues. Even more important, we would be demeaning ourselves as creatures made in the image of God if we gave up one of those characteristics that distinguishes us from all the rest of creation: our moral nature.

SO WHO'S TO JUDGE?

Chris had finally come to a conclusion. Her sister was doing wrong in the way she treated her own kids. Chris had watched it for years: the angry outbursts, the unpredictable severity, the spankings that bordered on beatings. Worst of all, Chris could now see the effects in her niece and nephew. They looked almost hardened against their own mother and less able to interact as kids ordinarily do with other family members.

The day came when Chris, with great apprehension, confronted her sister. That moment was charged with fear and anger and shame—fear because Chris knew how her sister would react, anger because Chris had built up a silent mass of indignation, and shame because she knew she was breaking the family norm by raising a problem.

Chris's sister's response was not hot, but chillingly rigid: Who are you to *judge*? It's up to me how I raise my kids. They are *my* kids. Chris doubted herself. What made me think this was any of my business? Fortunately, Chris sought the confidential advice of a friend who was a child therapist. Her objective information helped Chris decide that she was not making a mountain out of a molehill. She knew she could not let her sister shut her down with a simple accusation of being judgmental.

When and how should we judge the actions of others? How do we know when we are being fair judges of ourselves?

In any orderly society there is a system of courts, judges, and juries that can handle any judgments that need to be made. It is no different in our personal experience. We have to discern. We need to make judgments about ourselves and about others.

Fortunately, like the judicial system, we have multiple levels of judgment so that we can make clear decisions. There is the personal court (the conscience), the social court (the opinions of others), and the divine court (God's perspective).

Some people are virtual strangers to these courts. They've not taken responsibility for their actions their whole lives. For others these courts seem too threatening to approach. This might be the person who is wrapped up in shame and who cannot bear the thought of being evaluated. Yet that is what they are doing to themselves all the time. The real problem is that they bring a certain assumption to the process, a prejudgment. Because they *assume* they are always the guilty party, they never enjoy the relief of working through a situation and realizing they did the right thing.

The Conscience

Sometimes we picture the conscience as some imp-
ish figure sitting on our shoulders whispering words
into our ears. We think of it as a voice, and yet our consciences are, of course, not external to us. Conscience is
moral sensitivity, the ability to sense a conflict in ourselves when our attitudes or actions do not correspond
to our values of what is right and wrong. We say, "let
your conscience be your guide," and yet we need to be
careful. While conscience is a gift of God, it, like all
other human characteristics, is not infallible. It is only
one court among others that helps us judge our actions.

Consider the statement of the apostle Paul who was
being, in his opinion, unfairly judged by his critics:

> *I care very little if I am judged by you or by any human
> court; indeed, I do not even judge myself. My conscience
> is clear, but that does not make me innocent. It is the
> Lord who judges me. Therefore judge nothing before the
> appointed time; wait till the Lord comes. He will bring to
> light what is hidden in darkness and will expose the mo-
> tives of men's hearts. At that time each will receive his
> praise from God (1 Cor. 4:2-5).*

These comments have tremendous implications for
the issues of guilt and shame. Notice the points Paul
makes: we will be judged by others; the judgments of
others may or may not be right; we should be careful
even of our judgments about ourselves; we should
strive for a clear conscience; however, having a clear

conscience does not absolutely guarantee that we are innocent; God is the only ultimate judge of our actions; in this life we may not know with complete certainty whether a particular act was the right thing or not; someday we will know where we did right and where wrong; and at that time we will be vindicated by God.

The conscience, like the mind, has tremendous capabilities, but it needs to be trained and taught. That is where the social court and the divine court come in.

The Opinions of Others

How tricky this one can be! The social courts in which we move can give us terribly mixed signals. Think of something you want to do, and if you try, you can probably think of someone who you could count on to condemn the idea, but you could also find someone who would endorse it and affirm you in it. If someone decides to get a divorce, that person knows full well whose advice to seek to get the desired opinion.

Here too we are faced with amazing opposite attitudes among human beings. Some people do not care what anybody else thinks about them. They've always heard criticism—much of it deserved—and it is like water off a duck's back. Then there are those whose entire lives are determined by the opinions of others. They are constantly reading others: Do you like me? Did I say the wrong thing? What could I do to make you like me more?

Authority figures from our past have profound af-
fects on our views of right and wrong. Parents have a
tremendous privilege in shaping the moral lives of
their children. On the other hand, a child who wit-
nesses his father's habitual drunkenness may have no
twinge of conscience whatsoever about using drugs. A
child raised in a legalistic home may always feel
ashamed while listening to secular music.

Yet we need not be cynical. The counsel of others is
an absolutely indispensable court in which to try our
ideas and actions. What matters is *whose* counsel we
seek. If we are genuinely interested in evaluating ourselves we will seek out mature and honest people who
sense an obligation before God to deal with us in truth.
Paul thought this was possible. When the Corinthian
Christians were suing each other in the public courts,
Paul challenged them to take more responsibility as a
community to judge themselves:

> *Do you not know that the saints will judge the world?
> And if you are to judge the world, are you not competent
> to judge trivial cases? Do you not know that we will
> judge angels? How much more the things of this life!
> Therefore, if you have disputes about such matters, ap-
> point as judges even men of little account in the church!
> (1 Cor. 6:2-4).*

This is what the church of Jesus Christ is supposed
to be, and can be to us. There will, of course, always be
an ample supply of bad advice available. We have the
model of what kind of advisors to avoid in Job's coun-

selors, three men who made prejudgments and were bound and determined to find sin in Job's life. But there are in any Christian community, individuals who can be trusted as sound advisors. Not that they are the *only* court of opinion, but as a point of comparison of what we hear in our own hearts and what we see in the word of God. They are people who will confront us if we need confronting or comfort us if we need comfort.

When you are trying to sort out someone else's opinion of your actions, whether that person has concluded that you are innocent or guilty, ask yourself some simple questions about the source: Do I trust the judgments of this person in general, and do others? Is the advice consistent with biblical truth? What is this person's motive in giving me this opinion? Does this person understand both grace (mercy, acceptance) and truth (giving it to us straight)? Is this person qualified to give advice on this particular issue? Does this opinion correspond to the opinion of others?

Finally, we should be careful to get more than one opinion. Proverbs tells us that "plans fail for lack of counsel, but with many advisers they succeed" (15:22).

God's Perspective

Ideally the judgments that our consciences make and the opinions of trusted others will be reflections of God's truth. If we are prudent we will not necessarily assume that, but on the other hand we will not simply discard the signals we get from these two "courts."

Like the mind, our consciences need to be trained; like a group of students, those who have opinions about who we are or what we do are only as valuable as they have been taught by God.

Our immediate source for divine determinations of guilt or innocence is the word of God. Far more than a book of rules and regulations, the Scriptures are the very expression of the heart of God. When we read the Bible we find ourselves exposed to a searchlight from the heavens. While that causes some to run and hide for cover, others realize that it is better to be found than lost, and that a loving God will help us even in our guilt.

God and the Conscience

Psalm 119 is one of the best descriptions of how God, through the Scriptures, takes the external court of his righteousness and fits it into the conscience of the individual believer.

> *Oh, that my ways were steadfast in obeying your de-crees! Then I would not be put to shame when I consider all your commands* (vv. 5-6).
> Principle: Doing the right thing results in avoiding moral shame

> *I will praise you with an upright heart as I learn your righteous laws* (v. 7).
> Principle: The conscience is a learner.

I have hidden your word in my heart that I might not sin against you (v. 11).
Principle: Truth needs to be assimilated into one's innermost being.

I have set my heart on your laws. I hold fast to your statutes, O LORD; do not let me be put to shame. I run in the path of your commands, for you have set my heart free (vv. 30-32).
Principle: Freedom from shame is related to following God's paths.

Give me understanding, and I will keep your law and obey it with all my heart (v. 34).
Principle: A healthy conscience is a trained conscience.

I will speak of your statutes before kings and will not be put to shame, for I delight in your commands because I love them (vv. 46-47).
Principle: The conscience must face the challenge of discerning between what is shameful to others, and what is right.

Though the arrogant have smeared me with lies, I keep your precepts with all my heart. Their hearts are callous and unfeeling, but I delight in your law. (vv. 69-70)
Principle: Those whose consciences are hardened may be those who falsely accuse and impose shame.

Your word is a lamp to my feet and a light for my path
    (v. 105).
Principle: The conscience's tutor is the word of
    God.

I have strayed like a lost sheep. Seek your servant, for I
    have not forgotten your commands (v. 176).
Principle: We must not forget that we are constitu-
    tionally limited and fallible (natural shame),
    and need to be sought out by God.

At the core of the Christian gospel is the conviction
that in Christ, God has provided forgiveness from
guilt. "In those days, at that time…search will be made
for Israel's guilt, but there will be none…for I will forgive the remnant I spare," said the Lord through Jeremiah (50:20). Guilt nullified. Debt settled. This is not
Christian cliché. Dealing effectively with the objective
issue of guilt is the only hope we have for finding freedom from the experience of shame. Because Jesus was
"full of grace and truth," he reveals both the devasta-
tion of our sin, and the restoration offered through the
God of grace. Because his death was atonement, guilt
can be alleviated through confession and faith rather
than punishment.

Now that we have spoken of guilt and innocence as
objective judgments that we make—and need to
make—about ourselves and others day in day out, we
need to consider how all this works in our experience.

How do we deal with the feelings associated with guilt? How do we decide what course of action to take? But first of all, how should a Christian understand the way we function inside as thinking and feeling creatures? How should we react to the activities of our minds and hearts so that we will make good choices in life so that we will live rightly and well?

OVERCOMING GUILT AND SHAME

3

Thoughts and Feelings

Diane felt as if she had the weight of the world on her shoulders. Not only did she feel deep pain about her parents' divorce, her husband's stress-related medical problems, and her daughter's social difficulties, but she also experienced a sense of responsibility for these problems, a sense of judgment that seemed to convict her of some unknown wrongdoing. She felt lost and overwhelmed, questioning, What have I done? What should I do?

These painful experiences left her feeling helpless, without hope. Diane needed to have answers to her basic questions. Does she have guilt for her parents' divorce, her husband's medical problems, or her daughter's behaviors? What is her responsibility and what is not? Why does she feel so bad? To answer these questions, she will need to know and experience the difference between thoughts and feelings. Her feelings have alerted her to a problem, her thinking will have to guide her in knowing what to make of it all and what to do.

In our emotions we get impressions, in our thinking we develop judgments. Some people's experience consists primarily of painful feelings that seem to come from nowhere to torment them. To try to understand these feelings, they develop explanations for the emotions. Often these explanations include self-blame, self-accusations of having done something wrong because they feel pain. For others, thoughts dominate, and they appear to others as if they have no feelings. Yet they often experience a chronic, dull sense of uneasiness or inner pain that may motivate them to think harder, taking more control. Some people seem to be controlled by their feelings while others appear unable to have an emotion. There can be much confusion when people say, "I feel guilty" and "I feel confused," or, when asked how they are feeling, respond, "I was thinking..."

Some people place a kind of value judgment on thoughts and emotions. Thoughts are good, but emotions get us into trouble, is the message. Yet there is no warrant for considering either thoughts or emotions "good" or "bad." One is not "better" than the other. A biblical description of how God made us includes the full capabilities of both: we are to love God with heart, soul, mind, and strength (Mark 12:30). It is not that we deal with these *external* things called thoughts and emotions, it is the way we are. Consider the person of Jesus, who, as the divine Son of God but also perfect human, demonstrated both the logic and reasonableness of thought, and the surge of such emotions as compassion (Mark 1:41; 6:34), joy (Luke 10:21), anger (Matt. 21:12), and sorrow (Matt. 26:38). He comforted disciples with "troubled hearts" even as his own heart was "troubled" (John 12:27; 13:21).

Understanding the difference between thoughts and feelings can allow people to have a grasp on their own experience, to sort out what is happening, and to have a sense of self-control. When I can understand and label my thoughts and feelings, I can then make choices and change my experience. Being able to identify and respond to our thoughts and feelings allows us to resolve the pain, confusion, and sense of helplessness.

WHAT ARE THOUGHTS?

Thinking is an active mental process in which information is processed and conclusions are drawn. Determining guilt involves and evaluation of a decision made with regard to what is known and understood about a situation, what are believed to be the standards for right and wrong, and what is remembered about similar situations. These processes, such as decision-making, beliefs, and logical reasoning, involve thoughts.

Thoughts may evoke emotions. For example, a person who is remembering times with a good friend is very likely to simultaneously feel happy. In a similar manner, Diane, when thinking about her parents' divorce, is likely to experience emotional reactions such as sadness and anger.

WHAT ARE EMOTIONS?

We frequently refer to our emotions as feelings, the subjective internal experiences that are hard to define but give the flavor to our lives. Emotions are universal—all people have emotional reactions. We vary greatly in how sensitive we are in recognizing these feelings. While emotions certainly involve how we feel, they are much more than this.

Emotions may be described as a kind of internal weather. On some days, the sun gently warms our surroundings and floods our world with light, providing comfort and safety. On other days, storms cross over us, prompting us to protect ourselves. There is never a time when there is no weather, although our comfort with any given weather changes. In a similar manner, we are always having some kind of emotional reaction, although our awareness of and comfort with the emotion varies.

Our bodies are fully involved with emotional reactions. Physical arousal, or the changes which occur during a stress response, accompanies emotional experiences. These changes include increases in heart rate, respiration, blood pressure, hormonal secretion, blood flow distribution, and muscle tension. The degree of change in these physical responses is determined by the intensity of the emotional experience. All of these physical changes prepare the body for some type of action.

Emotions are reactions. They occur *in response* to something. We can learn to understand our emotions by identifying what the emotion is in response to, or the object of the reaction. We may ask the question: "What am I responding to?" An emotional reaction may result from something experienced in the present: a memory, a thought or belief, or even a sensation such as a smell.

Thoughts accompany emotional reactions. When we feel an emotion, we have thoughts that explain what we are feeling. At times, a thought occurs which produces an emotional reaction. For example, when we remember a time we were treated wrongly by some- one, we may feel anger, hurt, or shame. At other times, an emotional reaction may occur to a perception or sensation, which then results in a thought. The patient who leaves the doctor's office feeling shame may only later that the perceived disconnection due to the doc- tor's lack of eye contact.

Emotions have purpose. They provide information about what needs to change in order for us to cope with reality. We are always confronted with changes and we need to adjust. Our bodies are designed to adapt continually to changing situations and demands. Just as our eyes adjust when we walk out of a dark room into the sunlight, our emotions are designed to bring to our attention situations or beliefs that need to change. As we identify the object of our emotion, or the events or thoughts that caused the emotion, we can determine what must change. When we feel happy we are motivated to make many small changes so that the happiness continues. Telling a joke once may be funny; telling the same joke several times is not. Likewise, we are motivated to protect ourselves when we feel fear. The type of emotional reaction gives us information about what needs to change so that the situation may be maintained or improved, so we can cope better, or we can develop acceptance and adapt. The emotion is a signal.

Emotional reactions regulate the energy that is necessary to make the changes. Some reactions, such as anger, increase our energy so that we may change what is angering us. Other emotions, such as sadness, decrease our energy levels, slowing us down so that we may accept what has been lost.

The identification, acceptance, expression, and resolution of our emotions lead to changes within us. Our emotional reactions are resolved when we make the changes that are indicated by the emotional reactions. The experience of resolving our emotions facilitates internal changes in thinking and feeling that help us cope with reality.

Emotions provide us with information about our situation, regulate our energy to help us cope, and, when resolved, help us reorganize our inner selves so that we may cope better in the present. Our emotional reactions are thus an internal helper given to us by God to assist us in living. If we fail to resolve our emotions, we do not make the changes necessary to cope well, we experience changes in our energy level (often either agitation and tension, or fatigue and loss of energy), we may experience physical problems, and we develop chronic patterns of diffuse, unfinished business and feelings. Bitterness, depression, loneliness, anxiety, and hate may all result from unresolved emotions.

Emotions vary in both type and intensity. Each type of emotion has a name, has a distinct feeling, and provides unique information. Table 3.1 provides a summary of the names of basic emotions as well as the information the emotions provide. Other emotional reactions are combinations of these basic emotions. For example, frustration may be a combination of anger and sadness or anger and fear. The intensity of an emotional reaction varies. We may experience anger as anything from minor irritation to rage. In both situations, the anger indicates that we perceive something must change.

Table 3.1
Emotions and Their Purpose

joy, happiness: continue, this is good

acceptance, trust: affiliation, safety

anticipation: this is new, explore

surprise: this is unexpected, stop and get oriented, be alert *disgust, loathing*: this is "poison," push away, reject

anger: something is wrong or I have been wronged; I must change something in my situation or within myself to correct the wrong

sadness: a loss has occurred; adjust to the loss, adapt, accept

fear: danger is present; change the situation, learn either to cope or to escape from or avoid the situation

hurt: I have been harmed or abused; discontinue or avoid

shame: I am disconnected, I am not perfect; prompts repentance or reconnection, and acceptance of limitations, facilitating functioning well within reality; acceptance of real self

BRINGING THOUGHTS AND FEELINGS TO-GETHER

Diane has questions that deserve answers. Her feelings of shame, anger, fear, and sadness are strong and beg for resolution. As she sorts out her feelings, recognizing them as reactions that point her toward what needs to change, she began to feel less helpless and more helpful. Recognizing the difference between guilt and shame, she can acknowledge that she felt shame and then ask, "Where is the guilt? Who is guilty and who is innocent? Who is responsible and for what?" Her emotions direct her attention to problem areas and raise important questions. The answers to these questions provided a means for resolving her emotions.

People naturally develop thoughts that explain their emotional reactions. We fill in the blanks or develop an explanation for why we have the emotions we are experiencing. The emotional reactions and corresponding changes in energy provide much information; yet do not determine what is real or true. Rather, the emotional reactions draw us to something that needs to change. It is the interaction of our emotions with our thoughts that can determine what is real, what is true.

Sue was very angry with her husband Jim, believing that he had failed to act in a loving way toward her. If Sue can identify and accept that she is angry, she can use this to bring about changes so that her anger will be resolved. She may choose to share with Jim how she would like to be treated and inform him how he can act in a way that she experiences as loving. Or Sue may examine her own expectations and demands, and conclude that she has been unreasonable. This decision could lead to an acceptance of her husband's current patterns. She may combine elements of both. In any of these scenarios, change has occurred and her anger is resolved. Her emotional reactions directed her to address a problem and when she had made a sufficient change, the emotion was gone. Had she not acknowledged her emotional reaction and determined what needed to change, she would have likely developed a pattern of bitterness toward Jim.

If our explanations (thoughts) are accurate about the needs in the situation, we will experience either a continuation of positive emotions, such as happiness, or negative emotions, such as sadness. Some reactions may be maintained or changed very rapidly—such as fear subsiding soon after discovering that the noise heard at night is only the cat—while other emotional reactions, such as the grief experienced when a loved one has died, resolve over time. However, if our explanations are inaccurate or incomplete, our emotional reactions continue. Such emotional reactions prompt us to seek further change. Often the changes that produce emotional relief occur within us in the form of changed beliefs, demands, and interpretations that lead to acceptance and peace.

Our emotions direct us, helping us identify what needs to change so that we may live well. They also regulate our energy and provide motivation. On the other hand, our thoughts allow us to reason, to organize, to test reality and determine what is real, to provide a means of gathering further information, and furnish a forum for imagination, alternative understandings, and options. Our feelings of shame can direct us to identify where we are disconnected, where there may be guilt, and where changes need to occur. Our thinking is where we can make careful judgments about who is responsible for the disconnection, who is guilty. With our thinking and feeling, we are able to identify what we are feeling, determine what we are reacting to, and make decisions about how to resolve these feelings. We have the capacity to think and feel because we have been made in our Creator's image.

OVERCOMING GUILT AND SHAME

4

The Tutor: Moral Shame

Jeff knew what he needed to do. He just didn't want to have to do it. He thought that if he just ignored his feelings for a few weeks that they would go away. But he only felt increasingly uncomfortable around his parents. They had bought his story that the crumpled fender of the family car happened in the parking lot when he wasn't around. Fortunately, they hadn't seen the piece of tree bark stuck in the bumper, and they hadn't drilled him with questions because of their own suspicions. That only made it worse. They trusted him. They had a good and safe relationship in which everyone could be honest and straightforward. It was that, in the end, that had caused him to confess. The sense of disconnection from them was far more serious than the consequences of owning up to his actions. He knew he would feel ashamed either way—he just didn't want to drift farther away.

A young man comes to her pastor embarrassed and demoralized after finding out that after only a year of marriage, his wife has gotten into an affair with one of their best friends. He found out not by confession on her part, but through rumor. But worst of all is that she is showing no remorse about it. She gives no explanation, and doesn't appear to feel a need to. She simply dropped from sight in the church a month earlier when the revelations came, and is already making plans to move in with the other man. Her friends in the church have vastly different ways of sizing up the situation: She has just backslidden temporarily says the optimist; another wonders how committed she ever was to her husband or to God; still another says that no one should be surprised, after all, *anyone* married to *that* man would go looking for greener pastures. But who really knows what is going on in her conscience?

THE "FRIENDLINESS" OF MORAL SHAME

Shame is an emotion. Moral shame is what we feel when we properly sense that we have made serious mistakes or committed sin. It is when we feel disconnected because of what we have done, when we judge ourselves to be in the wrong. It is what we mean when we speak of a "guilty conscience."

This feeling of inner conflict or tension is the result of an inner comparison. It's as if we stand back, look at something we did or something we said, turn the other way and look at that internal set of standards or values that we have adopted in life, and we see a contradiction. It is the child who steals the toy of another, hears the internal voice of parents who have said it is wrong to steal, and then either corrects his actions or hides them. It is the mother who realizes her anger has driven her to the edge of abusing her children. It is the executive who hears a sermon on Sunday about not bearing false witness and on Monday gets a sale because he lied about his competitor's product.

These, of course, are the easy examples. It does not take a great deal of moral reflection to know when you've broken one of the Ten Commandments. We often have to face much subtler judgments: Was I wrong for confronting my mother about her drinking problem? Am I guilty of invading privacy and stealing because I confiscated some cigarettes I found in my teenage son's dresser drawer? Did I do something wrong by accepting cash from the person who damaged my car so that the police would not be called in on the situation?

Moral shame is a kind of tutor. In ancient times a tutor was a teacher, but much more than a teacher. He played the role of a guardian, looking out for the overall development of his dependent. Just so, God has given us this emotional ability to sense inner contradictions between moral standards and behavior. It is the correction that we need because of our tendency to get off track. Or as Paul told the Galatians: "The law was put in charge to lead us to Christ that we might be justified by faith" (3:24).

We sometimes do not like to hear the voice of our teachers, especially words of correction. Students sometimes respect their tutors, and sometimes do not. Human nature contains that impulse to be entirely self-sufficient. Besides, who *wants* to feel shame? It is precisely at this point that we have a very important decision to make. Will I seek a set of values and standards that will guide me in life, that will also curtail my desires and impulses, or will I make up the rules as I go?

That question may appear one way when we feel constrained (properly) by standards of right and wrong. That is where the temptation to muffle moral shame is the greatest. It's much easier to apply the rules of life to the other guy than to ourselves. But when we stop and think of it, how could we bear to live in a world where people made up the rules as they went? How would we be protected from the impulsive behaviors of others if nobody paid attention to any rules? How chilling is the last verse of the book of Judges in the Old Testament: "In those days Israel had no king; everyone did what was right in his own eyes."

Not everyone who feels ashamed is experiencing moral shame. If you are reading these words about responsibilities and rules and feel a sense of despair because others have told you that you should not "feel guilty" about so many things that are not your responsibility, you might be a person who is struggling more with *imposed shame* than moral shame (which we come to in the next chapter). You may have exaggerated the "rules" of life into an oppressive regime that nobody is able to live up to (that is what the apostle Peter had to tell certain people who wanted to take a "rule-keeping" approach to God. "Why do you try to test God by putting on the necks of the disciples a yoke that neither we nor our fathers have been able to bear?" (Acts 15:10). This is the challenge: We need to talk about our genuine moral responsibility, and accept moral shame as a friendly tutor pointing us in the right direction, at the same time, we need to see that some people feel ashamed because somebody else has improperly heaped it on their heads. Moral shame and imposed shame both *feel* the same, but they are categorically different experiences requiring totally different responses on our part.

WHERE DOES MORAL SHAME COME FROM?

Moral shame does not materialize from thin air. It is the response of a human being who has acquired a set of standards and values. To be a creature made in the image of God means numerous things, but it clearly includes our moral nature. Only human beings wonder about good, better and best, right and wrong, ought and ought not.

The ability to blush or bend your head is thus not a negative, but a sign that we are indeed unlike any other creature on earth. Your dog might bend his head when he wets on the floor, but probably only because he fears retribution. He does not lie awake at night with a troubled conscience. Your cat has no internal faculty for understanding the Ten Commandments, nor debate the ethics of having scratched your sofa beyond repair.

Human beings, created in the image of God, have this moral sensitivity that makes them capable of living not just good lives, but right lives. But sensitivity on its own is not enough. The moral standards we hold, have been put there by someone else. There are indeed numerous contributors to the moral development of a person, sometimes in agreement, sometimes in conflict. They include parents, peers, and, for a Christian, the Church and the Holy Spirit.

The Influence of Parents

Parents have an awesome degree of influence when shaping of the internal lives of their children. To deny that is simply to ignore the fact that we learn from modeling, and that most people are exposed to vast numbers of experiences with their primary models, their parents. Psychologists study all the developmental aspects of growing up, including the birth and development of the moral self. The Scriptures recognize the positive power of the parental voice. "My son, keep my words and store up my commands within you. Keep my commands and you will live; guard my teachings as the apple of your eye. Bind them on your fingers; write them on the tablet of your heart" (Prov. 7:1-3).

They also teach that because they are fallible, parents can pass on a tragic heritage of sin: "[God] does not leave the guilty unpunished; he punishes the chil-

dren and their children for the sin of the fathers to the
third and fourth generation" (Exod. 34:7). The implica-
tion of this sobering passage is that flawed morality
may be imitated by subsequent generations, not that
innocent children are held responsible for the sins of
their parents (cf. Ezek. 18:20). Though it is not necessarily so, thieves frequently raise thieves, beaters raise
beaters, and alcoholics raise alcoholics.

Thus follows a very important principle: though
parents ought to nurture in their children a proper
moral order for their lives, they may also pass on their
own moral shortcomings.

We can all think of people who were raised in stable, moral families where there was a consistent and
deep set of values and standards, and it shows in their
lives. As they grew up they gradually grasped the obvious and subtle differences between good and bad,
right and wrong.

We can also think of plenty of people who grew up
in an environment of total moral confusion. The who
child sees his mother shoplifting or lying to daddy's
boss about why daddy is not able to come to work today; the child who is blamed by parents for the ten-
sions in the home or the erratic behavior of an alcoholic
parent; the child who overhears adult conversations
filled with hate and invective toward others. There is
no way that such situations will not produce moral
confusion such children grow up. We see it in its stark-
est form when we hear stories of teenagers committing
murder totally without shame, not simply because they
ignore the laws of society, but because they have no

ability to empathize with the sufferings of other human beings. Disconnected from the human race, they inflict pain because they just do not care.

There are others who have a helpful or hurtful voice in the shaping of one's moral life.

The Influence of Peers

Peers are often the standard whereby individuals shape their values and rules for life. The bottom line here is acceptance. Who does not want to be accepted? "If I don't do drugs or engage in sex," thinks the teenager, "my friends will reject me." That teenager may be right. Human beings do not want to be shown up by someone touting a "higher standard," and may thereby discard the "do-gooder." Peer pressure is a tremendous force to resist.

Peer pressure is as influential in the adult world as in junior or senior high school. For adults the real judgment of the rightness of our actions is the comparison we make with the behaviors of others, rather than with the law, the policies of the company, or the regulations of the IRS. "Sure I cheat on my taxes, but no more than the average person." The problem is that "average" human behavior is frequently substandard and sinful human behavior. While most people admit that they lie regularly, they still expect their political and religious leaders to always tell the truth.

On the positive side, if people surround themselves with people who have an adequate moral structure for their lives, they will benefit by the influence of positive models. How encouraging it is to see someone do "the right thing" and end up not worse off for it, but better.

The Influence of the Church

For Christians, the church represents a key supplier of moral structure. There are many adults who got a significant part of the moral foundation of their lives through the long and steady voice of truth that they heard in the church they grew up in. Along the way, pastors, Sunday school teachers, and other leaders left an indelible mark on the spiritual lives of those under their care.

Unfortunately, because the church is filled with imperfect people who frequently misrepresent God in their dealings with other people, it is possible for someone to have a bad experience in the church. Many adults reject not only the church, but also Christian faith and God himself because they saw a hypocritical or oppressive style of Christian faith in the church they grew up in. The severity of the parochial school teachers or the moral failure of their childhood pastor created only moral confusion.

Of course, God cannot be held responsible for the failings of those who represent or misrepresent him. To reject God or to give up on finding a moral structure for life because of the mistakes of others is to cut ourselves off from the very source of life and goodness. That is why we must always seek the most direct influence of God in our inner beings, the work of the Holy Spirit.

The Influence of the Holy Spirit

The Christian believes that God himself, in the person of the Holy Spirit, is there to shape and repair the moral structure of our inner selves. The Holy Spirit has the ministry of being the Comforter or Counselor (John 14:16, 26), but he also is the instigator of moral shame when it is in our best interest to experience it. That is what Jesus meant when he said "when [the Holy Spirit] comes, he will convict the world of guilt in regard to sin and righteousness and judgment" (John 16:8). In other words, the Holy Spirit, for our own good, will work inside us, activating our consciences when appropriate, so that we will sense the danger of pursing wrongful actions. Moral shame does not necessarily make life easier, but it makes it safer and it makes it good.

The truth of the Word of God is the substance of what the Holy Spirit plants in receptive human hearts. The Scriptures are not merely a long list of rules and regulations, rather, they are the expression of the heart of God. They show us not only what God hates and what he loves, but why. It is possible for someone to look at the Bible and only see its shell, but when the illuminating work of the Holy Spirit makes the Word alive in our hearts, our inner moral structure is changed and shaped. That will happen only as we have a constant exposure to the Word through personal reading and listening to the teaching delivered by reliable interpreters.

RESOLVING MORAL SHAME

Blessed is the man whose sin the LORD does not count against him and in whose spirit is no deceit. When I kept silent, my bones wasted away through my groaning all day long. For day and night your hand was heavy upon me; my strength was sapped as in the heat of summer. Then I acknowledged my sin to you and did not cover up my iniquity. I said, "I will confess my transgressions to the LORD"-- and you forgave the guilt of my sin. Therefore let everyone who is godly pray to you while you may be found (Psalm 32:2-6).

It is not easy to hide. Human nature may incline us to run away from our mistakes, cover them up, or remove ourselves from the situation; but in the end, the spiritual, moral, and emotional costs are very high. We end up having to hide from the error, from the truth, from ourselves, from God, and from others. That is why many people end up confessing after a long and wearying struggle, long after a simpler healing could have occurred.

That is also why we long for forgiveness. Some people have almost given up on the hope that they might be forgiven; others have forgotten what it is to offer forgiveness for someone else. Perhaps most of us, however, know that reconciliation is so right, and feels so right, that if we knew what to do in a given situation, we would do it.

In situations when we need to deal with moral shame, and thus, the need for reconnection with someone else, there may be as many as six steps involved:

1. Identifying who is responsible
2. Accepting responsibility
3. Owning the feelings
4. Confession
5. Receiving forgiveness
6. Restitution or correction

Identifying who is responsible

To acknowledge that there is a problem is one thing, to identify who is to blame, another. We might be tempted in some situations to minimize the problem, thinking, "So what?" "It doesn't really matter," "I didn't mean any harm." Such responses are not adequate when someone was really hurt: the wife who was humiliated by the belittling comments from her husband during a party; the neighbor who finds his mailbox clipped off by the student driver next door; the man who learns he was passed by for a promotion because his boss didn't like his religious beliefs. Only the person genuinely responsible for the wrongdoing must deal with moral shame.

Accepting responsibility

The beginning of accepting responsibility is when we sense it. God has created us as emotional creatures in part so that we would experience feelings that point out problems or potential solutions. We have accepted responsibility when we sense what we have done and make no excuses for it. Feeling moral shame is thus the first step in moving beyond our mistakes and sins.

We have all seen children who find out how useful that simple word "sorry" can be. They learn from their parents that they must apologize when they do something wrong, but they quickly find out that "sorry" can be used as a magic word to quickly get out of a sticky situation. Then the parent needs to figure out how to explain what it means to be "really sorry"—not an easy task necessarily, and not always an easy concept for adults either. There is a world of difference between being sorry for being guilty and being sorry for having been caught.

Ownership of feelings

Moral shame can be painful. To the extent that shame results from disconnection, it is always to some degree painful. In addition to the shame itself, we may be angry with ourselves, angry at the situation, hurt or afraid. The danger in working out moral shame is that we will so quickly want to avoid really sensing the embarrassment or humiliation that we will wall ourselves off from our feelings.

This is especially the case for those who struggle with the burden of imposed shame. Some people are emotionally worn down by the constant criticism of others and have to daily remind themselves that they are not to blame in the way that their accusers would like them to believe. Then, when that person who wrestles with imposed shame really does do something wrong, it is very hard to really own the feelings of moral shame. It is almost as if there is only so much shame they can deal with, and so they have a hard time dealing with the genuine moral issues in their lives. This scenario shows how important it is to deal with imposed shame (which we come to in the next chapter). To know assuredly in which ways you are *not* blameworthy is the way to be able to accept blame when appropriate.

Confession

The hardest part about confession is gathering the courage to do it. There is no one formula, although there are opening comments that can open the door for confession itself: "There's something I've got to tell you that isn't easy for me," or "I have to say something to you because I don't want there to be anything between us," or "I know you're not going to like this, but…" or "we both know that there's something we need to talk about." Confession should be a simple admission of in which aspect you think you were to blame. It is possible for confession to get entangled in a long explanation that starts to sound more like personal justification than taking blame. It is better to clearly state where you think you were wrong, your feelings of regret about it, and then let the other party respond. Confession is a clear expression of accepting responsibility for wrongdoing. It may end up then that you do indeed have an opportunity to explain the subtleties of the situation.

There are some circumstances in which it is best not to confess. If a man tells a female friend that he has been fantasizing about her and has used her as an object of lust, he may end up doing needless harm to her. In such a situation the person can still confess to himself and to God, or perhaps make himself accountable to another person.

We confess guilt to the person we offended, but even more important is the confession made to God. After King David committed adultery with Bathsheba he was struck down by his sense of moral shame: "My sin is always before me [...] let me hear joy and gladness; let the bones you have crushed rejoice" (Ps. 51:3, 8). He pleads for God's cleansing (vs. 7). David has grasped the cosmic significance of his sin: "against you, you only, have I sinned and done what is evil in your sight" (vs. 4). He was able to say both "I know my transgressions, and my sin is always before me" (vs. 3), and "create in me a pure heart, O God, and renew a steadfast spirit within me" (vs. 10). David knew that he could approach God for forgiveness from guilt and relief from the crushing impact of severe moral shame. How different it is in our contemporary society in which we pretend that sin is an outdated concept, shame is a neurotic condition, God is apathetic, and forgiveness unnecessary.

Receiving forgiveness

Believe it or not, it can be as hard to receive forgiveness, as it is to confess. Many of us just do not believe that He comes with a soiled conscience wanting to be purified, or, as it says in Hebrews, "let us draw near to God with a sincere heart in full assurance of faith, having our hearts sprinkled to cleanse us from a *guilty conscience*" (10:22). Whereas the Old Testament sacrificial system was unable "to clear the conscience of the worshipper," the blood of Christ will "cleanse our consciences from acts that lead to death, so that we may serve the living God" (9:9, 14).

Restitution or correction

In some situations the final step in dealing with moral shame is "making up" for damage that was done. A teenager may express his great regret for backing into the neighbor's car, but an apology will not pay for a new fender. There is a very good reason why in the Old Testament law there is a strong emphasis on restitution or correction, which is different from punishment. Punishment does not make up for an injury, but it may be possible to experience some healing through correction.

Of course, some experiences are so severe that there is no simple thing that can be done to correct a tragic situation: marital unfaithfulness, repeated drug or alcohol abuse, habitual gambling, physical abuse, to name a few. You cannot simply "make up" the cost of such drastic mistakes. Yet a commitment to long-term correction arising out of genuine moral shame can be the first step in rebuilding a life and rebuilding trust in a relationship.

The Psalmist said in Psalm 32 that he decided not to hide his guilt any longer. "I acknowledged my sin to you and did not cover up my iniquity. I said, 'I will confess...'"(v. 5). Then only could he experience the wonderful forgiveness of God, and find God "while he may be found." It all starts with listening to the conscience, activated by the sense of moral shame, an ally that is given for our own protection. To find God in the aftermath of sin and confession is to cleansed and released from moral shame.

5

The Deceiver: Imposed Shame

Janet could not say exactly what she had done wrong, but she knew she felt deep shame. It seemed everything she had done lately was wrong. Her mother frequently called and instructed her on how to do everything, from home decorating to childcare to how to please her husband. Hidden in this "advice" seemed to be a constant message of disapproval. Her mother-in-law responded in much the same way, only with different advice. Janet tried hard to please each mother, yet sensed she was never successful. She wanted to do the right thing, but she felt like she failed at every point.

Her husband seemed to care, yet was often irritated with the house not being perfect, Janet's one night out, and her emotional reactions. She tried to be more "logical" yet sensed that she failed.

Janet's teenage daughter now seemed so distant, so uninterested in her. Janet knew she needed to allow her daughter to grow up, yet wondered if things had to be this impersonal. Her daughter blamed Janet for being "too nosey." Her relationships with the younger children now seemed more tenuous. Even relationships at work and with other friends seemed shaky.

Janet knew she felt deep shame. She was confused, wondering, Am I guilty? She felt so bad. She thought, I must be guilty, it hurts so much. Disconnected, Janet could identify with Job when he said, "If I am guilty—woe to me! Even if I am innocent, I cannot lift my head, for I am full of shame and drowned in my affliction."

THE ANGUISH OF IMPOSED SHAME

The emotion of shame occurs when we experience disconnection within ourselves, from someone else, or from God. Any dictionary will point to a second use of "shame." As a verb ("to shame someone" or "to put someone to shame") it describes the behavior of a person acting in a manner that makes it likely another person will feel shame. The common phrases "shame on you" or "you should be ashamed" are examples of attempts to impose shame.

Imposed shame is the painful emotional sense of disgrace, humiliation, self-contempt, or self-exposure along with a longing to reconnect with another person. Imposed shame is felt when adults are plagued because they cannot live up to their parents' expectations, when children hate themselves because they live in abusive homes, or a woman who was sexually abused is disgusted with her needs and vulnerability. It occurs when a parent tells a child it would be better if he or she had never been born, or that they would have preferred a boy instead of a girl. Shame is imposed when a husband keeps his wife weak and dependent by constantly belittling her and causing her to doubt herself, or when a wife blames her husband for everything that has ever gone wrong in her life. It is the kids on the playground making fun of the appearance of the chubby, shy kid, and it is the teacher who never rewards accomplishment but only penalizes mistakes. Such shame is felt intensely, somebody else is doing something to push us away, to isolate us or disconnect from us. We feel imposed shame when someone else has wronged us, transgressed against us and we long to be reconciled or reconnected with that person.

WHERE DOES IMPOSED SHAME COME FROM?

Anyone might experience imposed shame because we all have a need to connect with others. As shame is resolved when we experience some form of reconnection, the experience of imposed shame is characterized by a longing to reconnect with the one who imposed the shame. We believe that if we can only have reconnection with the imposer, to please him or her or be accepted by him or her, we will have relief from the pain of the imposed shame. Shame may be imposed in many ways. Imposers of shame may or may not be aware they have caused a disconnection. They may not have intended to cause a disconnection. Imposed shame may occur even without awareness or intent

When we feel shame, we do not automatically know which type of shame we are experiencing. As all types of shame feel similar, it is our thoughts that help us identify the type of shame we are feeling. Our feelings do not identify who is responsible for the disconnection or the wrongdoing. The common statement "I feel guilty" only confuses the experience. Better to ask: Am I responsible for this shame? Did I do something wrong? These questions lead us to know which type of shame we are experiencing and why we need to change in order to have relief.

The painful shame feelings can direct us to take action, to make changes in our thoughts and behaviors, which will allow a release from the pain. The question of guilt is central to the resolution of the shame experience. To find a way out from under the pain and burden of imposed shame, we need to sort through what we are feeling, thinking, and who is responsible. If I am guilty, then I can do what is necessary to resolve my moral shame. If I am not guilty, then I will want to know how to get out from the burden of imposed shame.

The strong feelings of imposed shame often interfere with our ability to think straight. Our thought patterns get distorted and we sometimes reach faulty conclusions. For many, the experience of feeling shame causes them to personalize actions or statements of others that are not personal. For example, the young man who experiences shame when his mother says she won't be happy until she has grandchildren, is actually responding to the disconnection caused by his mother's attitude. He is not at all guilty, yet his wrong conclusion about responsibility may leave him judging himself as a failure and unworthy. Others may experience selective attention, only noticing the negative statements of others and not attending to compliments or affirmation. When we feel shame, we have difficulty thinking realistically.

Imposed shame may occur in many scenarios. Simply being ignored or neglected by someone can produce feelings of shame. In addition to the emotional reactions, thoughts may occur such as, "What did I do wrong?" or "Why am I not good enough?" Children who are neglected or ignored are likely to feel ashamed, unloved, unworthy, and insecure. Adults who are not respected or listened to are likely to have the same reaction. Being falsely blamed for someone else's problems, wrongdoings, pain, distress, or general circumstances produces imposed shame. The tired parent who is short with his or her children, the insecure and angry boss who takes responsibility for anything, or the parents who look to their children to make them happy or proud, all are likely to impose shame on those around them. Such people wrongly hold others responsible for their difficulties. If you live with such an individual you can almost certainly count on being shamed.

In a similar manner, the denial of responsibility by one person may impose shame on those who interact with that person. Spouses who are self-indulgent or irresponsible often leave the other spouse feeling ashamed and inadequate. Parents who do not fulfill their parental roles inadvertently place pressure on their children to fill in the gaps, or to assume the responsibilities the parents have neglected. The children likely sense that if they can assume this responsibility, they will increase the odds of connecting with their parents. However, no child can fill the role of an adult. Thus the child loses on two counts: he or she "fails" at bearing an adult responsibility, and his or her normal, healthy needs to be nurtured, protected, and cared for go unmet.

When a person is violated—for instance in the case of physical, verbal, sexual, emotional, or any other kind of abuse—that too is the imposition of shame. Such acts step over the line, intrude on the rights of others, and violate the boundaries of acceptable behavior. Most often, a person who has greater power or status than the other person causes the violation. The person with lesser power or status longs to reconnect with the other, yet was not responsible for the disconnection.

Such can be the case in the parent-child relationship. Children define their identity and self-worth through their relationships with their parents. When parents violate the needs of children, children end up feeling disconnected. Violations of emotional, verbal, physical, or sexual abuse may occur either actively or through neglect. In spite of the violation, the child still longs to connect with the parent, for children need parents in all ways (physical, emotional, mental, and spiritual). Being abused produces fear, righteous indignation, rage, and shame. Abuse is a violent form of disconnection. The painful violations of abuse do not erase the child's need to connect. Rather, the child, left in imposed shame, often idealizes the abusing parent even more, believing, If only I could be good enough, I wouldn't be treated this way. The disconnection only makes the child need the parent more.

Adult men and women who have been abused by their parents often are the most vocal defenders and protectors of those parents. They often place their parents on a pedestal and ascribe to them great qualities, as if they can do no wrong. These adults have great difficulty holding their parents responsible for anything, rather, they attribute any form of disconnection or shame to themselves. They perceive their parents as basically good, themselves as basically bad. Even thinking about the abuse that occurred may result in more intense shame and self-statements such as "I must really be a bad person to have such thoughts." If they would acknowledge the abuse, they would fully sense the disconnection and shame. To preserve an illusion of connection and to attempt to minimize the pain of the shame, people who have been abused often sacrifice themselves to protect their parents.

Shame may be imposed in more subtle ways. People who learn that what happens to them is not related to what they do often become fatalistic, depressed, even hopeless. Psychologists refer to this as *learned helplessness*. Children need early in their development for their parents to respond to their sounds, then eye movements, and later, requests. They need to learn that they can impact their world, that they make a difference and can be seen and heard. In some families all behaviors are rewarded and praised, in other families all behaviors are punished, and in others the child's behaviors are randomly rewarded or punished. All three scenarios will result in imposed shame as such children experience disconnection from their parents.

In many seemingly "good" families, ego-boundaries between parent and child become blurred and confused. Emotional incest may occur in which the parent uses the child for the parent's emotional needs making the child almost a surrogate spouse. The child may appear to have a "special relationship" with the parent. Such a relationship denies the developmental needs of the child and thus pairs shame with his or her needs for privacy, independence, and autonomy.

Many individuals and institutions impose shame as a means of exerting control over others. The teacher who belittles a student, the spouse who can never be satisfied, the parent who is critical, the coach who insults and ridicules his athletes, and the pastor who only focuses on part of the gospel all are shaming others. Their behaviors are likely to elicit an emotional shame response in those around them and thus motivate those people to be compliant with the imposer's demands or wishes.

We can subtly impose shame on ourselves by reenacting or repeating the treatment we have received from others. Like a tape recorder that replays critical and humiliating messages from our past, our own thought patterns can condemn us even when we are not guilty, eliciting the feeling of shame when we reenact the disconnection we have had in the past. These thoughts may discount or minimize the positive and emphasize the flaws. We may hold ourselves to unrealistic expectations, demanding perfection. Or, we may project our shame onto others, inaccurately believing they have the same critical thoughts about us that we have about ourselves.

Our internalization of significant people can be of great value, as when one acquires the moral values of godly parents; then again it may be a curse, as when one hears parents who belittled and insulted. It *seems* like the shame is coming from one's own guilt, but in reality it is imposed shame, resulting from the historical disconnection experienced in prior relationships internalized in the past, and replayed in the present.

Imposed shame can cripple people; can inhibit them so that they appear to be merely a shell, a rough outer coating yet empty inside. The inhibitory effects of shame leave people bound up, unable to feel, and afraid to think for themselves. Distortions of reality, confusion, and the loss of the ability to think abstractly may occur with imposed shame. It is because imposed shame can cause such injury that Jesus said a person who calls someone else a fool is in danger of hell (Matt. 5:22).

Relationships are also impaired. The unmet need to connect leaves the shamed person highly dependent or fearful of others. Wanting to be loved, they are seemingly unable to receive love. God is often experienced as judgmental, harsh, and distant. Self-contempt and disgust or even hate and loathing of the self are not uncommon. Thoughts of being loved may occur but the feelings do not correspond. The failure of the imposer to reconnect with the one who was shamed leaves the hurting person feeling alone, unlovable, and helpless. The disabling effects of imposed shame are most evident in those situations in which there is a failure of the shaming person to reconnect with the one who was shamed. In such circumstances, emotions, thoughts, needs, talents, and even behaviors may become paired with shame so that the person lives in a chronic inhibited and painful existence. Unable to obtain relief from this painful emotion, this individual appears to be under the power of the imposer. (Appendix 3 summarizes some of the consequences of imposed shame.)

RESOLVING IMPOSED SHAME IS DIFFICULT

We might think that when people discover that they have been the recipients of imposed shame that they would immediately cry foul and shun its destructive and demeaning effects. The fact of the matter is that many, even after learning the distinctions between shame and guilt, moral and imposed shame, are reluctant to take action and deal with the shaming voices of the past. There are many possible reasons why someone might have difficulty dealing with their imposed shame, usually assumptions that are developed over a long period of time. Often, the fear of further shame or disconnection from the imposer, inhibit action. What follows are some of the most common beliefs that prevent people from dealing with imposed shame.

I feel so bad, I must be guilty

Confusing thoughts and feelings can lead to confusion over who is responsible. Our feelings of shame do not determine who is guilty; rather, the shame feelings direct us to identify that we perceive disconnection and prompt us to resolve the shame. In addition, the experience of imposed shame dominates our experience and intensifies the experience of moral or natural shame. Shame feelings that occur with our limitations or wrongdoings are added to the imposed shame, leaving us sensing that we are unforgivable or unlovable. Thinking in this faulty way, we conclude that we must be guilty in all circumstances.

It is wrong to blame

For some, dealing with imposed shame seems to contradict Christian values. It does not seem very "Christian" to blame others. Of course, Christian faith does place great emphasis on personal responsibility. But as discussed in Chapter 2, it is normal to judge the goodness, appropriateness, or value of our or others' behavior and determine who is responsible. Paul wrote in Philippians 1:9-10 "this is my prayer: that your love may abound more and more in knowledge and depth of insight, so that you may be able *to discern what is best* and may be pure and blameless until the day of

Christ." Shame resolution requires holding the guilty party, or the person responsible for the disconnection, responsible. This is simply the biblical notions of justice and discernment. If am the guilty party then my experience is moral shame. If the guilty person is someone else, then I am feeling imposed shame. Consistent with the great commandment (Matt. 22:37-40), shame resolution requires that we treat ourselves with the same love and respect that we show others.

The Past is the Past

We need to put the past behind us and move on. God is holy and righteous; he cannot ignore unrighteousness, and thus he has provided a means for resolving the sin within us. Made in God's image, we also cannot overlook injustices without a cost to us. While the disconnection or wrongdoing may have happened in the past, it is still affecting the present if we are experiencing imposed shame. Resolution will not be possible until we make peace with the past.

It is Wrong (Sinful) to Be Angry

Anger, as with any emotional reaction, may be misused. However, human anger can be righteous indignation following the example of God's anger. God is angry when he identifies unrighteousness or injustice. Our anger, when working properly, functions in the same way. It might be argued that there is something wrong with us if we do not have indignation at the malicious and wicked behavior of some people. Ephesians 4:26 assumes we will get angry: "In your anger do not sin. Do not let the sun go down while you are still angry." The principles for human anger resolution are (1) determine what is causing the anger; (2) address the cause directly; and (3) resolve it in a timely manner.

It Isn't Nice To Talk about Such Things

It's true. Many things that happen are not nice. Christians are not called to be "nice" but rather to love. The woman who says, "I can't let my parents know how their criticism of each other has hurt me because that wouldn't be nice," is showing love for neither herself nor her parents. In love, Jesus displayed anger, confronted those doing wrong, and exposed hidden secrets that were hurting others.

I Should Turn the Other Cheek

We must discern when to deal directly with a problem and when to exercise tolerance. Two principles apply. First, we are to love others as we love ourselves, meaning that God desires for us to value others and ourselves the way he does. Second, we are instructed to submit ourselves to each other. In the context of mutual love and respect, we can choose to submit. However, we are neither to overlook or ignore sin nor take on responsibility for what others have done.

I Am Instructed to Honor my Mother and Father

What does it mean to "honor" someone? When we honor someone, we show esteem and respect. Often, in order to avoid dealing with imposed shame we maintain lies or secrets about the imposer. For some, rather than showing honor toward their parents, they engage in a form of idolatry in which they do not love their parents as they love themselves, but rather, lift their parents to a god-like status, in which they can do no wrong. Honoring does not mean pretending that someone who is wrong is right. There is often great fear in dealing with things involving our parents: fear of disconnection from them or fear of changes within ourselves. It is, however, still possible to face difficult truths about your parents, and also honor them.

If I Resolve my Imposed Shame, I Won't Know Who I Am

We can develop an identity and lifestyle focused on trying to please or reconnect with someone. For many, their whole adult lives have been focused on trying to win the approval of parents. Schedules and vacation plans are built around them while other interests and opportunities are lost. When together, one wonders, "Are they okay? Are they happy?" and "If they're okay, then I am okay." The irony is that if the burden of imposed shame is taken away the person may need to find a new identity.

If I separate from the Imposer, I Will Lose My Self-Worth

Some people depend upon the very person imposing shame on them for their self-worth, even where there has been significant abuse. All children initially define who they are by identifying with and responding to their parents. When some form of abuse has distorted the parent/child relationship, it is common that the child is stuck in his or her development, unable to separate from the parent, yet unable to appropriately connect as well. To think of separating may be scary for it represents the loss of the hoped-for ideal parent.

It Will Hurt too Much

A person who experiences deep imposed shame often greatly fears emotional pain. Living in disconnection is painful. Emotional pain is not harmful, yet pain does hurt. Resolving imposed shame does involve experiencing painful feelings, but with the promise of new freedom from the domination of imposed shame.

I'll Be Responsible for My Own Life

Living under the tyranny of imposed shame may seem to excuse people from being responsible for themselves. Rather than decide how to live, what to value, or which choice to make, such people can do what they think the imposer would want. In this way, they stay small, childlike, and deny or minimize their own personal responsibility. They may seem to accept responsibility for others but actually are denying their responsibility in their attempt to please others. Some come to so identify themselves as victims that they resist acceptance and forgiveness.

If I Pursue the Truth, I May not Like What I Find

Being realistic may threaten idealized images of others. We may mistakenly believe that we need other people to be a certain way so that we will be okay. For some, the truth has been that they were abused, neglected, or wrongly taken advantage of, or not loved by their parents. For others, they may recognize that their parents really did the best they could and they were still hurt or their legitimate needs were not adequately met. We may loose the idealized family, spouse, friend, or even the image of who we hoped we were. However, acceptance and forgiveness provide a way toward peace, reconciliation, and resolution.

They (Those Who Imposed Shame) Have Changed; They Are not Like They Used to Be

If this is true it is good news. However, if in some significant way someone has inflicted imposed shame on another, the effects of that shaming still need to be resolved in the present. For some, the changes over the years in the imposers does allow for resolution if the issues are addressed.

I Cannot Hold Them Responsible; They Had a Horrible Childhood

It is true that what happened to us in childhood influences our adult behaviors. It is also true that we are not responsible for what happens to us as children because a child is never responsible for the behavior of an adult. As we become adults, we become responsible for our own actions and life. While we are not responsible for, nor can we control all that we experience such as painful feelings or memories, we are responsible for how we cope with them. It is true that most people who sexually abuse children were themselves sexually abused. However, it is also true that most people who were sexually abused do not choose to abuse others. Just as we have choices as to how we cope with our pain, memories, and needs, so does everyone else, including those who imposed shame.

If I Resolve the Imposed Shame, They Will Be Angry with Me

Sometimes people hesitate in dealing with imposed shame because of the reactions they anticipate in the imposers. Yes, the imposer may be angry. The anger of others does not harm us, although their behavior while angry may be dangerous. It is important that contact with the imposer occur at the appropriate time, a time when there is clarity of the issues, and when the confronter has all of their emotional reactions available.

I'm Afraid They Will Die

A common fear is that my honesty will harm the imposer. At times, the imposer may impose further shame, and thus inhibition, by making statements like, "It would kill me if I ever knew you were unhappy," or "You're wounding me" during expression of feelings or thoughts. It is important to have boundaries when communicating with imposers, recognizing that their actions are a reflection of their experience, not absolute and objective reality.

If I Confront This, They Will Reject Me

Yes, they may continue the rejection that has been occurring. Living in a relationship with unresolved imposed shame requires a denial of one's thoughts and feelings, disrespect for oneself. Many children learn to be quiet, denying their own feelings and thoughts in an attempt to connect with a rejecting or neglectful parent. Having not experienced, or having given up on true acceptance, the child and later the adult strives to avoid rejection. As such, people who are under imposed shame only have the illusion of being accepted. Their chronic feelings of shame and thoughts of inadequacy demonstrate they do not accept themselves. On the other hand, they may be accepted if they reveal their real selves.

They Will Only Pity or Patronize Me

Again, it is possible that the imposer will refuse to be vulnerable and will respond in a patronizing manner. If this is the case, it is probable that this is the status of the current relationship. Revealing the truth about our self creates the opportunity to be accepted while staying in the imposed shame patterns blocks any chance of being known or accepted.

They Won't Change

They may not change, or may even treat you worse. The only people we can change are ourselves. We cannot realistically expect others to be who we want them to be. But we can have freedom from the pain and inhibition of imposed shame, no matter what the imposer chooses to do.

SO NOW WHAT?

Knowing what we are experiencing helps decrease the fear, the sense of helplessness, and the feelings of being out of control. Being aware that we are not guilty even though we feel deep shame provides some relief. However, the disconnection that produced the shame may remain; the critical thoughts, feelings of self-contempt, and harsh judgments still weigh heavy on the heart. Knowing is not enough—emotional reactions require change so that they may be resolved.

Imposed shame is a spiritual issue. The full biblical concept of salvation is rescue or deliverance from our enemies. We are saved from ourselves in that God helps us overcome the mastery of sin and its penalty, but salvation is also a process of being delivered from external enemies. The work of Satan and the mischief of human enemies so often is the lie of false accusation. Our English word "devil" is the translation of *diabolos* (note: "diabolical"), which means "accuser" in Greek. This "father of lies," uses imposed shame to inflict harm. It should come as no surprise that there are so many people who have been beaten down and bruised with the blunt instrument of false accusation—imposed shame.

The same gospel of Christ that offers us deliverance from our guilt also proclaims that God does vindicate, and that he will reverse the effects of every false, destructive accusation. There are no guarantees that we will not be victims in this life, but the Scriptures invite us to a confidence based on the righteous judgment of God. When those who manipulate through shame try to shrink other people, to bend their heads down in shame, the truth and judgment of God may be the most important principles to apply. God will bring to light what is truly right and truly wrong.

While ultimate judgment is, of course, God's role, we still need to evaluate—to make judgments—about what is happening around us. Even common sense tells us that to protect ourselves we need to know when someone is mistreating us. Both Peter and Paul said that though people around them were trying to make them ashamed of what was right (the gospel), they refused to bow to the injustice of it all (2 Tim. 1:12; 1 Pet. 4:16). This too is part of living as moral creatures.

6

Resolving Imposed Shame

The healing of imposed shame begins with awareness and concludes with reconnection between ourselves, God, and, in some form, those who imposed the shame. Mere awareness does not provide relief and may actually increase the pain. It is necessary for the emotional reactions, thoughts, and judgments based on reality to work together to relieve the pain, address the needs, and move toward reconnection and resolution. Resolving imposed shame is a process that involves the whole self. In some situations, the imposed shame can be quickly identified, understood for what it is, and released by acceptance or boundary setting. For example, dissonance felt when encountering a person who says "You should be ashamed of yourself," when you choose to stay home with your sick child instead of going to work may be resolved by deciding that your actions are correct and the other person, the imposer, is wrong. Accepting this may release the shame. Many, if not most, situations of imposed shame are much more difficult to resolve. To resolve our imposed shame in situations that involve ongoing relationships or historical events, we need to be realistic in our thoughts and understandings, active in responding to and resolving all our emotional reactions, and we need to build relationships that are realistic and respectful of all people involved.

THE PROCESS OF RESOLVING IMPOSED SHAME

Resolving imposed shame is a process that happens over time, involving our thoughts, emotions, behaviors, and relationships. The healing process involves the following steps:

1. Identify and accept the presence of shame.

2. Attribute responsibility for the disconnection.
   a. Hold yourself responsible for your part.
   b. Hold the other person responsible for his or her part.

3. Identify, own, and resolve all emotional reactions.

4. Use anger to reestablish boundaries.

5. Learn to accept love.

6. Apply love to self.

7. Confront the imposer (in person or symbolically).
   a. Confess personal responsibility.
   b. Identify the responsibility of the person imposing shame.

8. Forgive and be forgiven.
   a. with respect to the other;
   b. with respect to yourself;
   c. with respect to God.

9. Rebuild the relationship in truth and grace.

Healing from shame does not follow a cookbook
list of "how to." Rather, resolving shame involves addressing your particular needs at a particular time in
your life and in light of the particular situation. The
process of imposed shame resolution involves these
nine steps that we pass through at different rates.

Identify and Accept the Presence of Shame

What am I feeling? Some can quickly identify
shame as deep pain, a sense of being exposed, and
thoughts of inadequacy and unworthiness. For others,
shame inhibits their feelings, leaving them numb and
believing that they are helpless or deserving of their
plight.

The pain, the desire to hide, and the accompanying thoughts of inadequacy and unloveability all point to shame. Feelings of embarrassment, disgrace, or unworthiness also signal the presence of shame. An avoidance of or discomfort with eye contact, a lowered head or drooped shoulders and increased physical distance from others signal the presence of shame. Self-critical and obsessive thoughts may dominate. These experiences indicate the presence of shame—but they do not identify the type of shame.

Attribute Responsibility for the Disconnection

What type of shame am I feeling? Who is responsible? We determine what type of shame we are experiencing by figuring out who is responsible for the guilt or disconnection in the relationship. If I am guilty, then the experience is moral shame and I can try to resolve it as described in Chapter 4. However, if I am not responsible for the disconnection, and if I am not guilty, then I am feeling imposed shame.

The same thinking processes that determine if I am guilty are used to determine if someone else is responsible for the wrongdoing or disconnection. Jesus instructed us to love others as we love ourselves. In determining who is responsible, I must assess both my behavior and that of the other person. I need to hold myself responsible for my actions and hold the other person responsible for his or her actions. To hold others responsible is not wrong, it is in fact, one way of respecting others as we respect ourselves.

If we fail to hold others responsible for what they have done, we cannot progress further. There cannot be acceptance, forgiveness, or release of the shame unless there is an accurate attribution of responsibility. I cannot forgive people who have wronged me unless I recognize that they have wronged me and hold them responsible (no matter what their intent was). It is only then that I am able to forgive them. In other words, the only way to offer the gift of forgiveness and of reconciliation to others is first to hold them accountable for what they are responsible for. This "holding responsible" sometimes occurs occurs in our thinking such as when a confrontation is not advisable or not possible, as for example, when the imposer is deceased.

While I am not responsible for the things others do or have done to me, I am responsible for how I cope and live now. I am responsible for how I care for myself and how I treat others. I may realize that I have been victimized--others have wronged me. However, my identity is not to be that of a victim but of a full person. All of us are more than what someone else has done against us.

Identify, Own, and Resolve All Emotional Reactions

Once we determine who is responsible, we are likely to have many emotional reactions. Shame often functions like a blanket covering other emotions. This inhibition contributes to the pain and the sense of helplessness, but is broken when we determine who is responsible. We may feel fear at any time in the resolution process, since it may seem dangerous or wrong to hold another person responsible for what they have done (or are doing). We may be afraid of what will happen next, what will happen if the imposer discovers what we are thinking, or what will happen if we change. We may feel sadness when we recognize what has been lost, or the way things could have been. If we recognize these losses we may feel the hurt of the past that was never resolved, which may be the beginning of a necessary grieving process.

We may experience anger as we become aware of wrongdoing, injustice, unfairness, or mistreatment. We may feel disgusted with the entire situation. The anger and disgust may be against both the person who imposed shame and ourselves. The anger may work against acceptance but working through the anger will help us recognize and accept reality.

Use Anger to Reestablish Boundaries

Anger has another important function. Shame resolution may require a reestablishment of the boundaries that were violated when the shame was imposed. We need boundaries. They provide a sense of who we are; they define the thoughts and feelings that are unique to us. Our boundaries are like an old farmhouse with many rooms, windows, and doors. Some of the rooms are for everyone. Both family and guests may use them. Other rooms are only for family and some only for private use. One is a workroom, another a playroom, while yet another is an intimate bedroom shared only with a spouse. We make choices as to who is admitted into what room. We choose when they come and leave. An attic and basement exist for storage of things that are not often needed but remain available. Some items in storage may have been there a long time and the owner may have forgotten that they ever existed. The doors and windows allow the owner to make adjustments for safety and privacy. They may be opened to let something either in or out.

In any given situation, we have choices as to what room within us we will allow any specific person access to. Many grow up in families were children are not allowed to separate from their parents, and believe, often unaware, that they do not have the option or right to limit what rooms their parents or others can enter—the child who was always made to submit to the kisses of departing relatives, and then had no internal boundaries available when an uncle began to sexually molest them. Lacking options for privacy and safety, they view themselves more like a warehouse with no walls or windows.

Getting angry when we realize that a boundary has been violated helps us to rebuild the walls within us so that we can make choices regarding how to relate to others. We need the option to say "no" in order to be able to say "yes," to give, or to choose to submit. Feeling anger tells us we need make a change, to establish a boundary, to set a limit. Our anger gives us energy to make the changes, and the anger can then be released when the boundaries are set. In future contacts with the person who imposed the shame, the anger can be available to immediately set the boundaries, should they be threatened. In doing so, further problems may be avoided.

Learn to Accept Love

Setting boundaries is necessary, yet may leave us lonely. Shame blocks our ability to receive love from others. Furthermore, many who have experienced imposed shame have not had many opportunities to receive real love; for the love offered has been accompanied with a hitch, a hook with conditions. One woman, after visiting her mother, reported she felt like she had received a "hug with a slug." Confused as to what real love is, this woman knew that what she had been offered left her feeling inadequate and unlovable. Setting boundaries is necessary, but not sufficient, for we all need to be loved.

Before we can give love we must receive it. We cannot give what we do not have. God is the ultimate source of love, as recorded in I John 4:19: "We love because he first loved us." When imposed shame covers the self it may be difficult to receive God's love. It is not at all surprising that people struggling with imposed shame commonly feel distant from God and his love. Learning to receive love must occur within relationships. The shame was imposed in relationships: the healing will occur within relationships. These relationships may occur with friends, in support groups, in therapy, or in other loving relationships.

While under the influence of imposed shame, accepting love is difficult if not impossible. The person who is covered by imposed shame feels the pain of disconnection, self-contempt, isolation, and is not able to receive love. The attempts of others to extend love may be misinterpreted and pushed away. The messages that occurred in the disconnection are paired with the emotion shame and replay automatically. Messages given, either overtly or covertly, maintain the imposed shame. It is as if the imposer is continually present, repeating the disconnection.

Learning to receive love from others counters the shaming messages. If someone is able to love me, then I may be lovable. If someone connects with me, then I am able to connect. The acceptance of love from another contradicts the messages and validates the person's anger at the imposer. This is how others can reflect God's love to a person trapped in imposed shame. The messages of the imposer are proven wrong by love. Choosing to allow others into the rooms within us that have been covered with shame opens the opportunity for us to be accepted and to be loved. As we expose the imposed shame, the shame loses its power and we become more free to experience the emotions that have been hidden under the shame blanket. Learning to receive love from others counters the shaming messages. If someone is able to love me, then I am lovable. If someone connects with me, then I am lovable.

Apply Love to Self

The way we think and feel about ourselves is largely determined by the treatment we have received from those around us. Like a reflection seen in a mirror, we initially develop our identity and self-esteem through our interactions with our parents. Children learn to think and how to feel about themselves according to how they have been treated. Later in life, friends, peers, and media all provide a reflection of who we are. As we experience others loving us we are handed a new mirror in which we can see our reflection. At this point, we can choose to apply to ourselves the love others are offering.

Receiving love and then applying this love to ourselves, dispels the messages of worthlessness and self-contempt. We begin to see beyond the pain of the imposed shame. This opens the opportunity to know firsthand the experience of being loved. Self-esteem is now possible. Genuine self-esteem occurs when shame is resolved. Until then, we are not capable of being good enough or perform well enough to have stable self-esteem or to be loved. Our performance is inadequate. Self-esteem will naturally be there when imposed shame is removed from us and we accept ourselves as God views us. All the people struggling to build self-esteem through this or that method may be failing because what they really need is to deal with shame in all its forms.

Confront the Imposer

With a more realistic perception of ourselves, acceptance of our own emotional reactions, and understanding of who is responsible, we are ready to address the imposer. We may be afraid to confront. Whether the meeting occurs in person or symbolically, we need to first share our understanding of the situation, including who is responsible; and second, confess our sin (if we have guilt in the issue). The imposed shame is released to the imposer. Most importantly, the confrontation must be tempered by love and truth.

The purpose is to allow for the possibility of reconnection. Acceptance is key to the process. Acceptance involves an emotional embracing, and a release of hopes and expectations for, or claims against, someone or something. The man who accepts his father comes to grips with the reality of who this man is (or was), his strengths as well as his faults, what he has done, and what he failed to do. In like manner, to accept ourselves requires the same awareness of who we are—the good and the bad. Acceptance means seeing others and ourselves as God does.

At times, a face-to-face meeting is not possible. The imposer may refuse to address the issues, may not be safe to meet or to be vulnerable with, or may be deceased. At such times, the "empty chair" technique can be helpful. We can imagine that the imposer is sitting in an empty chair and can share our thoughts, feelings, and requests as if the imposer were present. It is often helpful to have a safe and trusted person present to share the experience, and witness what occurs.

We must also, in a sense, confront the internalized voice of impose shame within us. Here, it may be necessary to symbolically confront the imposer. The man who hears his father tell him, "You're not good enough" or his mother's voice saying, "You're still my little boy," must confront those messages, identify that they are not true, direct his anger toward the false nature of the messages, and replace them with true thoughts about himself. He may find it helpful to carry with him a card on which he has written true self-statements (see Appendix 4). Or, he may imagine that Jesus is confronting the imposer and that he can rest safely with Jesus. When the internalized voices begin to impose shame, our anger can energize us to confront the lies and replace them with the truth. Thus we may find the mixed-up broken parts inside us coming together or reconnecting. We may find it easier to connect with God as the barriers of imposed shame are knocked down.

Forgive and be Forgiven

In forgiveness is hope for the resolution of imposed shame. Forgiveness is not merely forgetting or making excuses for what happened to us. Avoidance of conflict or a compromise in our moral position is not evidence of forgiveness. Events, behaviors, or words that have caused disconnection or harm have effects. Like a scar that results from a wound to the skin, forgiveness heals the wound but does not necessarily remove the evidence.

Forgiveness involves letting go, a cancellation of a debt, a release, a pardon. The New Testament word for forgiveness (aphesis) simply means letting go or releasing. Forgiveness is choosing not to punish someone though justice affords that right. Created in God's image, we capable of experiencing righteous indignation when we have been wronged. Forgiveness is recognizing the wrong, holding the person who has transgressed responsible for that wrong, and, in light of this, choosing not to punish. Forgiveness is the application of grace and truth: truth in that the wrongdoer is held responsible; grace in the offer of love and release. Forgiveness provides a bridge, a way for the offender to be reconnected with the offended. The offender (imposer) may request forgiveness; the offended may offer forgiveness. While many emotions are involved before, during, and after the forgiveness process, forgiveness is primarily cognitive. The offended person makes a decision or a commitment to release any claims against the offender. The process of forgiveness then involves applying this choice to whatever circumstances may arise. The living of forgiveness challenges the person who has forgiven to continue to release the offender each time there is a reminder of wrongdoing. Confronting our imposed shame and the person who has imposed the shame offers an opportunity to take the shame off ourselves and place it on the appropriate person. Confronting allows us to let go of what is not ours, what we cannot change, and give it back to whomever it belongs, who is the only person who can deal with the guilt. So Ezekiel says, "The soul who sins is the one who will die. The son will not share the guilt of the father, nor will the father share the guilt of the son. The righteousness of the righteous man will be credited to him, and the wickedness of the wicked will be charged against him" (18:20).

Only the person guilty of imposing shame can resolve his or her guilt; the innocent party cannot. We are able forgive because we have been forgiven by God ("Forgive as the Lord forgave you," Col. 3:13). As it is not possible to give a gift you do not first possess, it is difficult to forgive anyone without first accepting forgiveness from the source of grace and truth. Any offer of forgiveness is not cheap. God recognizes both our proper desire that justice be served, that wrongdoing not go unpunished, and the desire to be reconciled to our enemies. Paul wrote in Romans 12:18-20:

> *If it is possible, as far as it depends on you, live at peace with everyone. Do not take revenge, my friends, but leave room for God's wrath, for it is written: "It is mine to avenge; I will repay", says the Lord. On the contrary: "If your enemy is hungry, feed him; if he is thirsty, give him something to drink. In doing this, you will heap burning coals on his head."*

Paul notes that there are limits to the degree to which we can live at peace with others. It simply is not entirely under our control. He clearly states that retribution and judgment will happen, though this is God's role and not ours. All the victims of this world will be vindicated, not by their own actions, but ultimately, by God's.

A boy grew up without a father because his father was killed in an auto accident in which his blood alcohol level was twice the legal limit. As a young adult, he had many feelings regarding the loss of his father. He was angry that his father was such a heavy drinker, that he had chosen alcohol over the family on many occasions, and, to make matters worse, that he was a "mean drunk." The boy was angry that he had to go through life without a father. By God's grace, he had come to peace with these losses. He had chosen to let God deal with his father in God's perfect wisdom, righteousness, and grace. His father had already faced God. Knowing this, the young man could release his desire for revenge or punishment and allow his grieving to occur, accepting the losses and embracing his own status as a son of his heavenly Father.

We can forgive; in fact we need to forgive, whether or not the imposer requests forgiveness. Those who impose shame do not have the power to block the forgiveness of those whom they have shamed. This does not mean forgiveness is easy or uncomplicated. What if the confession was half-hearted (e.g., the adulterer who was "caught")? What if the other person is confessing something he or she has confessed a hundred times before (e.g., the alcoholic who does more damage to the family with each failure)? What if the person confessing has a superficial understanding of how devastating the transgression was (e.g., the husband glibly who apologizes for striking his wife)? The more complicated the situation, the more work it will take to come to resolution. It may require the counsel of a third party, a pastor, or a counselor. Nonetheless, the principle remains the same: to forgive is to let go and let God be the final judge—which he is anyway.

Frequently those who impose shame deny their responsibility. Thus the shamed person is confronted with a choice; namely: Whom do I believe? We need to be prepared for several possibilities. The imposer may not care that the wrong occurred, may conclude that the issue is unimportant, may be angry that someone is holding him or her responsible, or may disconnect further in an attempt to impose further shame and thus inhibit the process. At such a time, the shamed person needs to hold on to what is true and receive support and love from others.

There are other possibilities. Convicted of sin, the imposer may accept responsibility and apologize. At times, the conviction occurs immediately; in other circumstances, much time passes before the imposer returns and requests forgiveness. Again, it is the shamed person's responsibility to forgive the imposer whether or not the imposer acknowledges forgiveness. Forgiveness allows us to be released from the power of the imposer as well as from our own moral shame and bitterness.

Sometimes we may perceive that we were wronged when we actually were not, and thus it is not appropriate to offer forgiveness. At times, shame may be experienced, a disconnection is felt, and yet nobody is really guilty of doing wrong. For instance, there may be an honest difference of opinion, yet no one is responsible for a moral transgression. Misunderstanding a difference in preference may lead to a sense of distance or disconnection and the emotional reaction of shame. If a husband and wife ridging together in a car differ in their preference for listening to music, they are not facing a moral issue; yet if their expectations were not clear or accepted, one or both individuals could experience disconnection and thus shame. There are times in which we need to forbear instead of to forgive.

Rebuild the Relationship

Speaking the truth, realistically and with mutual love, addressing responsibility, and forgiving permits the beginning of a new relationship between the shamed person and the imposer. This new relationship can be built in truth, each person being honestly accepted. However, forgiveness does not erase consequences, nor does it destroy memory. The new relationship, built in grace and truth, is characterized by respect for all involved.

At times, mutual respect allows for increased openness and intimacy. Releasing shame grants the opportunity for people to know each other, to come out of hiding, and to heal. However, in other circumstances it is neither safe nor wise to become more vulnerable to the imposer. The physically abusive husband who denies wrongdoing and threatens further beatings if "I ever hear another word of this" is not safe.

A new relationship with someone who has already died is possible. Although the imposer is dead, the living person maintains a relationship with the imposer through memory and emotions. A new relationship in memory is then necessary, a relationship built in grace and truth. This new relationship in memory will alter the shamed person's perspective not only on the imposer, but also on himself or herself. As we are able to realistically accept ourselves and others, we become more open to God.

BRINGING IT ALL TOGETHER

The resolution of imposed shame can be a lengthy process that changes the very heart of the person who has felt the shame. Kathy found this to be true. A divorced woman with a young son, Kathy felt inadequate and unlovable. She was aware that she had always tried to win her father's approval. On one occasion, the birth of her son, she felt as if she had succeeded. Upon her divorce from an abusive and adulterous husband, Kathy received increased criticism from her father. She sought counseling after seriously considering suicide. Over time, she learned to experience herself more realistically, separating herself from the harsh and untrue messages given to her by her father. She built relationships with others who reflected her true value. After much prayer, she decided to share with her father how his criticism hurt her.

To her dismay, he blamed her for her own pain and refused to acknowledge any responsibility. Kathy was now confronted with forgiving him for this rejection. She turned more to her Heavenly Father and released her claims against her earthly father. Forgiving him included her adjusting her expectations of him.

A few years after the meeting with her father, Kathy shared that she still longed for a father-daughter relationship and that at times, she felt the grief of this loss. Yet she no longer felt bitter toward him nor motivated to either please him or resist his control. With her imposed shame resolved, she experience true self-esteem and had peace and acceptance of her identity in Christ.

OVERCOMING GUILT AND SHAME

7

Clay Vessels and Natural Shame

After we have accounted for moral shame (the experience that follows a real failure or transgression), and imposed shame (the experience that results from someone else's judgmental or condemnatory behavior), there still remains a form of shame that lingers in the background. It is not necessarily connected to any specific thing we do, and it does not come from an outside source. It is, rather, that sense that we are by nature limited, fallible, and frail. It is the knowledge that, though we might try to do our best, make all the right choices, and say all the right things, we will not. It is not an oppressive experience, and in many ways it is a feeling not to be shunned. We may call it natural shame, because it arises out of our nature as creatures who are made in God's image, but are sinful and fallen, affected by all the limitations and digressions that life presents us with every day. It is, to put it one way, a "milder" form of shame because it is not experienced as a crushing load or a malicious voice. Yet it has in common with all the other forms and degrees of shame that sense of disconnection from another, of being incomplete and imperfect

Natural shame is often experienced at times of contemplation, self-reflection, or solitude. We may experience natural shame when we are frustrated, disappointed, or let down, even though we feel we have done our best. It may occur when we are making plans or reviewing life goals. Acknowledging that we cannot give anymore, try any harder, or perform better may be a threatening experience if our sense of worth or acceptability is directly linked in our minds with performance.

NATURAL SHAME AND REALISTIC EXPECTATIONS

Joe and Nancy wanted to be the best parents in the world. It took eight years before they were able to have their first child, so the three children that they eventually had were truly cherished. They had spent plenty of time talking about how they would nurture, discipline, and teach their children. Though their love for their kids never faltered, Joe and Nancy did struggle with things not being as perfect as they had hoped. Their children had problems like other children, and Joe and Nancy themselves were finding shortcomings within themselves as well.

They were embarrassed of themselves when they lost their temper with their kids. They regretted times when they misinterpreted a problem or applied an inadequate solution. They swallowed hard when they had to apologize to their own children.

When they sought the council of trusted and mature friends they were told that they were indeed very good parents, and that they were normal. Yes, they would make mistakes, but what parents don't? Joe and Nancy found themselves having to adjust their expectations of themselves and those of their children. They did not want to lower their standards; neither did they want to content themselves with something less than their best effort in raising their family.

Natural shame is that humble acceptance of our constitutional limitations as human beings. It is accepting reality. It is that sense that people have, that they are incomplete creatures that live in an incomplete world. It is what Christians mean by "fallenness," and what they accept as a biblical view of life. We do fall short; we are fallible, frail, and limited. It was not our created nature, but it is what human nature has become. The unnatural has become natural. The person with an appropriate grasp of natural shame will say, "I will try my best today, but I will not live a perfect life. I accept the fact that I will have to apologize to people and to God throughout my life, because I know I will never be perfect in this life. If I hide from my natural shame I will only set myself and others up for disaster because I'll not be living in reality." It is that general sense of humility that comes with maturity and wisdom.

THE BENEFITS OF NATURAL SHAME

To accept our fallenness and fallibility is in many ways the key to understanding how to rise above it. The humility of natural shame, therefore, is not a sense of defeat or hopelessness about life, but the beginning point to finding the life-giving grace of God. It takes away any presumption that we can make ourselves perfect. The motivation behind perfectionism often is the desire to rise above shame by sheer personal effort. The futility of such efforts is the reason why the perfectionist lifestyle appears so hollow. God has reached out to us not because we are near perfect, but because of how far short of perfection we fall.

Natural Shame and Other Forms of Shame

If we can understand the dynamic of natural shame in our lives we will better interpret the instances of moral shame and imposed shame. Some people, for instance, will rarely admit to mistakes or transgressions. They seem to have hardened consciences—they have no moral shame. Not surprisingly, that person will usually be a stranger to natural shame as well. Somewhere along the way such people come to believe that they are not morally responsible, but, sadly, to others they merely look amoral or immoral in attitude and behavior. What has happened is that a person thinks he is more than what he is. He is non-responsive to the voice of moral shame, and thus he will go on in life hurting people, limiting himself, and dishonoring God.

On the other hand, the person who has the humility of natural shame will not be surprised when moral shame comes knocking. That person will say: "There goes my conscience again; but why should that surprise me, I know I will sin and my conscience is here to speak to me and protect me from repeating the same mistakes."

Natural shame will help us understand the imposers of shame in life as well. Natural shame means we see ourselves as sons and daughters of Adam and Eve, and admit that ever since the first generation, human beings have blamed others for their mistakes (cf. Gen. 3:12-13) and have developed all kinds of ways to impose shame. Natural shame helps us to understand that people who is belittle or demean us are also members of a fallen race and are only showing one of the severe forms of fallenness in their hurtful behavior.

Natural Shame and Lifelong Needs

Shame, in all its forms, points to disconnectedness. Natural shame is there in the background to continually remind us, among other things, that we dare not let ourselves drift free of other people. In a world where isolation, alienation, and loneliness are so often the norm, we need a longing inside us that will drive us to the supply. Natural shame can take the form of a kind of hunger for relationships.

More importantly, natural shame reminds us of our need for something and someone bigger than ourselves. We need God. That is in part what the apostle Paul was pointing toward when he said, "I do not understand what I do. For what I want to do I do not do, but what I hate I do . . . As it is, it is no longer I myself who do it, but it is sin living in me. I know that nothing good lives in me, that is, in my sinful nature. For I have the desire to do what is good, but I cannot carry it out" (Rom. 7:15-18).

Here is a man with a significant sense of natural shame. Yet that is precisely what drove Paul to find a way out, a solution found in Jesus Christ: "What a wretched man I am! Who will rescue me from this body of death? Thanks be to God—through Jesus Christ our Lord!" (vv. 24-25).

RESOLVING NATURAL SHAME

Unlike moral shame and imposed shame, we resolve natural shame not by dealing with it and moving beyond it, but by accepting it. We need to be open to the reminders of natural shame throughout our lives, that while we live with great God-given privileges, we also live with natural limitations. Dependence upon God is a necessity, not an option. When the Scriptures encourage us to be humble (cf. Prov. 15:33; 18:12; Zeph. 2:3; Col. 3:12; Tit. 3:2; 1 Pet. 5:5; etc.), they are instructing us to remember that in this life, at any moment, on any day, we may stumble.

Paul put it this way: "We have this treasure in jars of clay to show that this all-surpassing power is from God and not from us" (2 Cor. 4:7). God has given an absolute treasure. The gift of life, even in a fallen world, is a value beyond measure. What is more, to be living creatures made in his image is a privilege almost beyond imagination. Yet these treasures are placed in simple clay jars. The Genesis equation is that God took the dust of the earth, added to it the breath of life, and humanity resulted. Even before the human race fell, it was made of clay. *Adamah* (Hebrew for "dirt") plus *ruach* ("spirit") equals *adam* ("man").

Our bodies are clay jars. Sometimes that is where we sense our frailty the most. For the shameless person who goes through life arrogantly and proudly it may be his only encounter with pain, physical frailty, or death that finally shows him that he is not invincible. People who struggle with new or chronic physical handicaps, disease, or infertility may deal with a sense of shame—certainly not moral shame and probably not imposed shame—but most likely the shame of feeling disconnected from their bodies. In their feebleness they sense their limitations.

Our inner selves are clay jars as well. Bodies can and do break, and so can our interior lives of emotion and thought. Your heart may be broken by the death of a loved one. You may have felt that common sense of powerlessness when he or she was dying, and a tearing disconnectedness when that loved one finally did die.

Another person tries not to be hurt when that boyfriend or girlfriend ends a relationship, but the heart shows its fragility. People deal with weakness of mind all the time: the adrenalin of test-taking anxiety, the frustration at not being able to understand technical parts of a job, the shame of getting more forgetful in older age, the pain of depression that does not subside even when the person knows all the right answers. We are clay.

This is to take nothing away from the benefits of salvation. When God says, "I will accept you," he is extending his saving hand to a creature who is fallen, and who (although renewed and restored in sanctification) remains a member of a fallen race. We are not saved because we are perfect or even because we are made perfect, but we are saved in spite of being imperfect.

There is good news in being made of clay. We are clay vessels, but vessels that are uniquely shaped by God; and made for the purpose of containing his eternal treasure.

This is worth pondering carefully. Two of the major prophets of Israel—Isaiah and Jeremiah—repeatedly used the image of God as the potter and us as the clay. "Yet, O LORD, you are our Father. We are the clay, you are the potter; we are all the work of your hand," said Isaiah (64:8). "Th work of your hand." That is the important part. Our lives began with the creative work of God, and they continue only by the sustaining hand of God. From the day we were created, we were dependent; and with sin in the world and in us, we are even more dependent.

Despite the problems of guilt and shame in us, we are still vessels capable of containing God's eternal treasure. What does that mean? It means that God is at work in human hearts, bringing about the really good things of life through them—spiritual blessings of love, joy, peace, patience, kindness, goodness, faithfulness, gentleness, and self-control—if we have the humility, sometimes inspired by natural shame, to know that he is the potter and we are the clay.

8

A Story

Guilt and shame are not merely abstract principles.
They are the concrete realities of ordinary people. They
are the unseen messages borne in our hearts. Helpful and
unhelpful forms of shame can arise at any time. They are
prompted by the relationships of the past and the pre-
sent — relationships with parents, friends and acquain-
tances, coworkers, spouses and children, and God. In
this complex web of relationships in which we all live, we
are left with the task to figure out, before God, who we
are and what we should do. We conclude this book with
an extended illustration of the dynamics of guilt and
shame.

The Monroe family, by any external comparison, was a "typical" family. They lived in the same kind of middle-class house as most of their friends and acquaintances; they looked like most of the people in their church; their teenage son and daughter were involved in the normal activities of their high school.

That was one reason why Gwen Monroe, the thirty-nine-year-old mother, hesitated in seeking someone else's counsel about her problems. After all, she was brought up in a "perfect" family. She was the apple of her father's eye and the joy of her overworked mother. She kept trying to convince herself that if she simply tried harder to be a better mother, a better wife, a better nurse, and a better Sunday school teacher—that her feelings of inadequacy and discouragement would melt away. They never did.

Nobody would give her anything other than an "A" for effort. Gwen was known as a responsible person who would never step on anyone else's toes, and who spent a good deal of her energy trying to help other people with their problems. Her kids thought she was a good mother, her pastor wished he could have ten more like her to teach Sunday school, and her supervisor treated her well in order to keep her with the hospital.

Only those closest to her—her family and two or three old friends—knew that she was in a continual inner struggle. Her way of coping was to keep moving. Activity was distracting. She was beginning to realize, however, that she was running very hard to keep a step ahead of an inner voice of condemnation, and that she was weary from the chase. The harder she tried, the more isolated she felt from other people. She knew it was time to stop trying to hide. She was near emotional collapse when her oldest daughter and husband insisted she seek help.

Her husband, Jeff, had the sense that he was in a wilderness of his own. Part of it was his relationship with Gwen. They had been married eighteen years, and he had grown very familiar with Gwen's emotional ups and downs. Trying to encourage her always seemed like pouring water in a leaking pail. He loved her very much, but was aware that along with his sympathy for her was a resentment in him that seemed to be getting more firmly rooted. He hated himself for feeling that way, but his self-condemnation did not lessen his latent bitterness.

The real spiritual and emotional crisis for him, however, was a secret he had borne for the past four years. He still could not really believe that he had committed adultery while on an extended business trip. When he thought about the incident, it seemed like looking at another person instead of himself. He did not drink often, but that night he did; he never thought about going to bed with another woman, but that night he had. It all seemed like the chapter out of someone else's life.

He never told Gwen because he thought it would destroy her. However, the more time passed, the more he wished he had, and the harder he thought it would be. He thought he had dealt with the issue with God. He remembered the tears of pain shed when no one else was looking. Yet he wondered if he was in the right spot with God. By not confessing to his wife, it

OVERCOMING GUILT AND SHAME

seemed like there was something hidden in the corner that was rotten and stinking. Had God forgiven him? When would He?

He was also at a point of growing frustration with his job. It seemed like he had reached a plateau. He had not gotten a promotion in the past three years, and there was no prospect for one. The job market for people in advertising was very tight, so he knew he was not going to find a similar position somewhere else. He felt like he was walking up a dead end alley. That made him wonder if he could have made better choices in his career. *If only I had taken the time to get that Masters Degree eight years ago when I had the chance,* he thought. *If only I had the energy of some of these people in their twenties who get the attention of management by their total immersion in their work.* He remembered when he was like that ten years earlier, and how he felt like he had almost abandoned his young family by doing so.

> *Sometimes we are aware that we are dealing with guilt and shame, and other times the signs are more telltale. Jeff knew every day for the past four years that an indiscreet and sinful act on his part had made him guilty. There were times when he almost wished God would inflict some pain on him, perhaps and illness, so that he could experience punishment and then the relief of it being over. No such punishment ever came. He felt shame for what he had done. He was not as aware, however, that he was experiencing shame also when he expe-*

rienced doubts over his career accomplishments, when he compared himself to coworkers, when he regretted not getting a graduate degree, and when he felt bad for being resentful toward his wife.

Gwen was entirely unaware that she was in a continual struggle with shame. Her experience was more severe than Jeff's. She almost always felt alienated or discon- nected from other people. Her attempts to perform were her way of gaining acceptance from the people in her life, from God, and from herself. She tried to do the "right" thing (which to her meant what made other people happy), so others liked her, but always wondered if there was a lot more under that constant smile.

Gwen debated whom she should talk to. She was not sure she needed professional counseling, so she decided to talk to her pastor at least initially. So many of her ups and downs were related to spiritual ques- tions: What does God want of me? Why don't I feel close to him? Why doesn't he answer my prayers? Jeff came along at her request.

The pastor let Gwen and Jeff do most of the talking for that hour. He asked a lot of clarifying questions be- cause Gwen's feelings seemed to relate to almost every aspect of her life. To every question the pastor put to Gwen she nodded without hesitation: Do you think people would reject you if they really know what kind of person you were? Do you very often feel like hiding, like crawling into a hole? Do you feel like your emotions are often numb or painful? Do you question your involvement in the Christian Education program or even being a member of the church? Do you sometimes feel like a failure in the other roles you play in your life: wife, mother, nurse? Do you oftentimes feel distant from God?

The pastor told them that he clearly sensed a common denominator behind Gwen's struggles: shame. Her attempts to hide, her sense of disconnectedness and inadequacy, and now her near emotional exhaustion pointed in the direction of a huge load of shame that she had been carrying for a long time. He explained the differences between moral, imposed, and natural shame, and observed that three factors pointed in the direction of imposed shame: first, there was no great unresolved transgression in the past that Gwen had avoided dealing with and that would have pointed to moral shame; second, her sense of shame followed not only the ordinary mistakes and failures in life, but at times when she was evaluating her looks, status, or performance; third, she remembered reacting this way to life since childhood.

After the talk and after doing some reading and Bible study Gwen felt a little overwhelmed, and Jeff sensed that a whole new door was opening to them. He also felt almost surgically opened after the discussion of moral shame. That's me, he thought. He realized that one day when things were more stable he would have to confess to Gwen.

*Realizing in a new way that guilt or shame are issues in
our lives is like coming back to a fork in the road. It may
mean looking in a new way at your thoughts and feelings, your actions, your values, your relationships, your
past. Any kind of change—even a change of perspective—can feel threatening or destabilizing. Yet when our
eyes are opened and we clearly see our guilt or our
shame, when we hear that ring of truth, we will do best
to not run from it all, but to embrace it, to understand it,
and to begin to deal with it. Such is the case for a person
experiencing imposed shame (like Gwen) or moral shame
(like Jeff). Acknowledging that that aching feeling we've
had so long is shame is the first step toward liberation
from it. We need to come to the point of being able to say:
"so that's why I've felt disconnected and isolated for so
long." We can then address the question of guilt head on,
discovering through the conscience taught by God and
by others whether we have guilt to be confessed, or false
blame to be rejected.*

After doing some reading and after two more meet-
ings with her pastor as well as serious discussions with
her husband, Gwen uncovered what she had known
deep down for a long time. All her agonizing about her
public presence, her performance in work, church, and
home, her looks, all her anxiety over every little interaction in every relationship all pointed to a treadmill of
shame on which she was caught. She was able to admit
to herself that she had been hiding behind a fake and
fragile smile, but that she was really profoundly un-

happy inside. She confided in two friends, but found different reactions. One seemed interested in understanding, while the other acted as though Gwen was saying things that were taboo.

For Gwen herself it was especially difficult to look at her past. She had heard the horror stories of those who had been abused in childhood, and for a while she feared that maybe that was her story but she just didn't remember it. Through the help of a Christian counselor, Gwen concluded that that was not her situation, but that some subtle dynamics in her growing up years had molded her into the super-responsible but insecure adult she was.

Gwen knew that her home life as a child was difficult. Now she learned that her mother's emotional struggles were a chronic problem with depression, maybe even manic-depressive illness. Her mother would drop out of sight for days at a time, leaving Gwen—the oldest child of four—the one responsible for taking care of the family. Gwen had gone further, and felt responsible to try to keep her mom happy, and took it personally when she was not.

How unsettling it can be to begin to look at your life from an entirely new perspective. A totally new perspective on people and events from our past can be unsettling, but necessary.

Gwen felt something new and frightening, however, when she recalled how her father had insisted she
take that role, that she be almost a surrogate spouse in
the absence of her mother, hearing his problems, giving
him advice—how could he expect a ten-year-old girl to
act as an adult? She felt angry. She could now see that
he tried so desperately to keep his wife's mental illness
a secret that he used his children to hold his own life
together. It was no wonder that now as an adult and a
mother herself she had been living a dual life: the responsible outer self and the agonizingly shameful inner self. But as soon as anger came, shame overwhelmed her. My mother couldn't help herself and
what was Dad to do? After all, he didn't beat us or
some such thing. She fought back and forth with her
emotions for the next few months as she tried to grasp
the truth of her life. Coming to grips with her feelings,
then moving past them to the truth was the hardest
thing she had ever done in her life. In the end she realized her mother was ill and her father simply made
bad choices by placing on Gwen's shoulders a load she
was not equipped to carry. Gwen regretted that she
could not attempt to reconcile with her father. He had
died two years earlier. Yet, in a way, she felt more reconciled toward both of her parents than ever before.

*Most of the significant people in our lives wear neither
white hats nor black hats. Gwen had only fooled herself
into thinking that her parents could do no wrong. But
neither would it do to make them the darkest of crimi-*

nals. Gwen needed to come to see that people helped shape her life, and that included the mistakes of her father.

Gwen ended up with a whole different outlook on life. Instead of being carried along by her shame, and instead of shame putting words in her mouth and determining her actions, she was able to pull herself back from her shame, call it an emotion, and act appropriately. She still felt the stabs of shame, but she was capable of holding off on judging her actions until the full strength of the emotion had passed. Furthermore, she ended up being much more capable of handling moral shame. When she did make a mistake or sin, she was able to feel regret and remorse without plunging into despair. Ironically, when she had been trapped in imposing shame, she never dealt adequately with her real faults. She used to avoid real moral shame because she simply did not know what to do with it.

Eventually, Gwen understood the phenomenon of natural shame. It was very hard for a life-long perfectionist to admit her natural fallibility; but this, in the end, was nothing short of liberation. She let go of what amounted to "righteousness through works," and instead, grasped the steady and sure grace of God. For the first time in her life she felt like she understood what it means to be a child of God.

CONCLUSION

The Cross of Christ:
Focus of Shame

We come finally to the crux of the matter. "Crux" is the Latin word for cross. The cross of Christ is indeed the meeting place—the crux, or crossroads if you will— where the life-threatening problems of guilt and shame meet the overwhelming power and grace of God. In- deed, the final word on guilt and shame belongs to God, for in the cross of Christ is provided the one effec- tive solution to the problem of guilt, and all the forms of shame that issue forth from it.

There is one compelling reason to believe that God has decisively dealt with sin and guilt, and will deal with the shameless perpetrators of human pain—it is that God himself stood in the spot of the greatest shame ever experienced in the universe, and in so do- ing, began the work of unraveling the guilt and the shame that has beset the human race since Adam and Eve.

We observe three ways in which guilt and shame were central to the drama of the crucifixion of the Son of God: (1) Christ took the punishment appropriate for the guilt of humanity, so that human beings would not have to take it themselves; (2) he experienced what was inherently foreign to him: the moral shame of humanity; and (3) the ridicule, derision, and rejection that his crucifixion represented was the ugliest moment of imposed shame ever perpetrated in history. Indeed, Christ came specifically for this purpose, to pay for the guilt, and to nullify the shame that in every generation has pushed human beings further from God.

There is one pivotal biblical text in which revelation comes full circle, from innocence, to shame, to the reconstruction of broken humanity:

> *Let us fix our eyes on Jesus, the author and perfecter of our faith, who for the joy set before him endured the cross, scorning its shame, and sat down at the right hand of the throne of God. Consider him who endured such opposition from sinful men, so that you will not grow weary and lose heart (Heb. 12:2-3).*

The "joy set before him" was Jesus' vision of once guilt-ridden people becoming cleansed. He saw to the other side of forgiveness, and so he endured the cross. It was worth the pain. By an act of love greater than the world had ever seen or will see, he was willing to be seen as the incarnation of guilt itself (2 Cor. 5:21). He was willing to be accused, and convicted, and humiliated, even put to shame so that we could gain freedom. In fact, because Jesus was the only human being who had no reason to experience shame, voluntarily taking shame was a sacrifice of infinite worth.

How did Jesus scorn the shame of the cross? By triumphing over it. Granted, this is the experience of the unique Son of God, but at the same time it is the path that was blazed for. He put shame in its place. He let us know that while shame has been central to the human story, it does not have to be its concluding chapter. Moral shame is only a passageway to confession and forgiveness, and imposed shame is only the sting of the lies and deceptions of others. If truth is an eternal principle that God enforces, then the pain of imposed shame will inevitably fade before God's righteous gaze.

Appendix 1

WHAT ARE GUILT AND SHAME?

"Guilt" is the objective state of being responsible for a wrongdoing or transgression. Guilt is not an emotion or feeling; rather, guilt is the status of being in the wrong. Its opposite is innocence. Guilt is independent of one's experience. For example, one may be guilty and not be aware of one's guilt, or one may believe that one is guilty but actually be innocent.

"Shame" is the subjective, personal, and painful emotional experience that occurs when one feels disconnected. It is a painful awareness of feeling inadequate, unworthy, and exposed. When we feel shame, we often feel inhibited, or as though we want to hide. Although all shame feels essentially the same, shame has three distinct forms:

"Moral shame" is the sense of remorse or shame felt when one judges that he or she is responsible for a transgression, or wrongdoing; when one is responsible for some disconnection. God uses moral shame to help

us identify the wrongdoing, know limits, and facilitate reconnection with Himself and with the person who has been wronged. It is what we mean when we speak of having a "bad conscience."

"Imposed shame" is a sense of shame that is imposed by one person on another. Someone else is causing the disconnection. Imposed shame may feel the same as moral shame, but it has a different cause, namely, someone else's behavior. The intent of the other person is not relevant to the experience of imposed shame. Some situations in which imposed shame may occur include: the denial or misattribution of responsibility by another, abandonment or neglect by another, or in situations of emotional, mental, physical, or sexual abuse. Repeated imposed shame over time can profoundly affect a person.

"Natural shame" is the sense of being fallible, limited, or frail. It is a result of the disconnection between the human race and God. We experience natural shame when we sense that we are unable to be perfect, and may not be known fully or understood by others. We may sense natural shame at times of reflection and in situations in which no specific transgression has occurred and no specific person is responsible for the disconnection. The humility of realizing our natural limitations is important in living responsible and safe lives.

Appendix 2

The Resolution of Shame and Guilt

Shame is resolved when reconnection occurs. While all shame feels similar, the type of shame can be identified by the following question: "Who is responsible for the disconnection?"

If I am responsible for the disconnection, then I am feeling moral shame. Moral shame is resolved through dealing with guilt and the reconnection with the one who was wronged. Moral shame resolution involves:

- acceptance of personal responsibility
- ownership and the resolution of the other emotional reactions involved in the situation
- confession of the wrongdoing
- acceptance of forgiveness from the other, God, and self
- restitution or correction as is relevant in the situation.

If another person if responsible for the disconnection, then the experience of shame is imposed shame. Imposed shame resolution involves the following steps:

- reattribution of responsibility, i.e., holding the proper person responsible for his or her actions and accepting responsibility for one's own actions
- identification, ownership, and resolution of all emotional reactions in the situation
- use of anger to reestablish ego-boundaries
- acceptance of love from another person
- application of love to the self
- confrontation of the other person (either in person or symbolically)
- confession of personal responsibility
- acceptance of forgiveness from God, the other person, and one's self
- rebuilding the relationship in truth

If no specific transgression has occurred and fallen human nature is responsible for the disconnection, then the experience is natural shame. Natural shame is resolved through an acceptance of God's reconnection with us through Jesus Christ and our acceptance of redemption and grace.

Appendix 3

ANATOMY OF THE EXPERIENCE OF SHAME

Characteristics of the Shame Experience: Healthy Dimensions

- sense of humility and need for God
- embarrassment over breaking social norms
- realistic understanding of personal imperfections
- responsiveness to internalized morals & values

Characteristics of the Shame Experience: Unhealthy Dimensions

- fear of vulnerability & exposure of self; a sense of waiting to be found out
- feeling like an outsider, disconnected, lonely
- defensiveness
- perfectionism
- fear of intimacy & commitments
- impairment of friendships; may look to rescue others

- getting stuck in dependent or counter-dependent relationships
- shyness, feelings of inferiority or worthlessness often resulting in social withdrawal
- anger, jealousy, and judgmental attitudes toward others
- difficulty in accepting forgiveness
- feeling distant from God
- legalistic ways of thinking
- use of compulsive behaviors to block feelings
- use of excuses, rationalizations, lies
- blaming others
- self-centeredness or selfishness
- exaggerated sense of personal flaws or ugliness
- sense of powerlessness and inability to change
- depression and even suicidal tendencies

Appendix 4

TRUTH STATEMENTS FOR CHALLENGING IM-POSED SHAME*

Is imposed shame an issue for you? How do you react when...

- you look in the mirror?
- you make a mistake or fail at something?
- you succeed and receive acknowledgment or praise?
- you receive a compliment?
- you are disappointed in someone?
- you are aware that others are disappointed in you?
- you are angry with someone?
- you are aware someone is angry with you?

If you find yourself feeling ashamed in such circumstances, imposed shame may be an issue for you.

The following statements can be used to confront thoughts or messages from others that impose shame.

It may be helpful to write out the statements that are most meaningful to you and carry the statements with you. When you are distracted or disturbed by the pain of imposed shame, reviewing such truth statements may be very helpful.

1. God knows me and he loves me.
2. God has said he will help me.
3. It is good and right for me to love myself as I love others.
4. I am fearfully and wonderfully made.
5. It's okay to ask for help.
6. Just give it a try—it's okay if it's not perfect.
7. It is okay to cry—Jesus did.
8. It is okay to be angry when something is wrong.
9. If I've made a mistake or hurt someone it is okay to apologize.
10. It's okay to be different.
11. It's okay to try something new, to experiment.
12. I can try something creative—I have a worthwhile ideas.
13. It is okay to have needs—God made me this way.
14. If I don't understand something, that's okay, I can ask for clarification.
15. It's okay to be scared—I can know God is with me.
16. Jesus will never leave or reject me.
17. God also gets angry when people hurt other people.
18. My sexual feelings and drives are given by God.

19. I don't have to struggle alone—I can ask for help.
20. God will give me his strength when I am weak.
21. The more I share the closer people feel to me.
22. It's okay to say no.
23. If someone seems untrustworthy or hurts me it's okay to back off.
24. It's okay to have fun.
25. It's okay to relax—I need to be refreshed and replenished.
26. The truth is always my friend, even when it is painful.
27. I can make it through my pain—God will be with me.
28. It's okay to rock the boat.
29. It's okay to speak the truth in love.
30. I may have been alone when I was young but I will make sure I won't have to be alone now.
31. Just because someone is angry doesn't mean I'm bad.
32. Being angry at someone doesn't mean I don't love them.
33. It's okay to grow up and separate from mom and dad.
34. I don't have to try to make everyone happy.
35. The problems in my family of origin were not my fault—I was a child.

*Ingrid Lawrenz, M.S.W.

Appendix 5

SOME KEY BIBLICAL REFERENCES REGARDING GUILT AND SHAME

- When I feel like no one knows me or loves me: Ps. 139
- When I feel unprotected: Ps. 31:1
- When I know I need to confess sin in my life: Ps. 32:2-6
- When I perceive a disconnection from my mother and father: Ps. 27:10-12
- When I feel like avoiding my past and myself: Ps. 51:6
- When I think I should not separate from my parents: Gen. 2:24
- When I mistakenly think my feelings of shame mean I'm guilty: Job 10:15
- When I mistakenly think I am responsible for the actions of others: Ezek. 18
- When I fear I will be abandoned by God: Phil. 1:6; Josh. 1:5
- When I have trouble trusting God: Ps. 119:137; Deut. 33:27; 2 Chron. 16:9; Ps 139:1-6

- When I want to take revenge: Rom 12:17-21
- When I feel I am the worst sinner: Rom 3:23
- When I feel like my forgiveness won't make a difference: Matt. 6:14-15; Mark 11:25; John 20:23; Col. 3:13
- When I feel like I can't be forgiven: Matt. 26:28, Mark 2:7, 10, I John 1:9
- When I think I shouldn't take action when I've been wronged: Luke 17:3